Cambridge Elements ☰

Elements in Ethics
edited by
Ben Eggleston
University of Kansas
Dale E. Miller
Old Dominion University, Virginia

BUDDHIST ETHICS

Maria Heim

Amherst College, Massachusetts

D0841746

CAMBRIDGE
UNIVERSITY PRESS

CAMBRIDGE
UNIVERSITY PRESS

University Printing House, Cambridge CB2 8BS, United Kingdom

One Liberty Plaza, 20th Floor, New York, NY 10006, USA

477 Williamstown Road, Port Melbourne, VIC 3207, Australia

314–321, 3rd Floor, Plot 3, Splendor Forum, Jasola District Centre,
New Delhi – 110025, India

79 Anson Road, #06–04/06, Singapore 079906

Cambridge University Press is part of the University of Cambridge.

It furthers the University's mission by disseminating knowledge in the pursuit of
education, learning, and research at the highest international levels of excellence.

www.cambridge.org
Information on this title: www.cambridge.org/9781108706629
DOI: 10.1017/9781108588270

© Maria Heim 2020

First published 2020

A catalogue record for this publication is available from the British Library.

ISBN 978-1-108-70662-9 Paperback
ISSN 2516-4031 (online)
ISSN 2516-4023 (print)

Buddhist Ethics

Elements in Ethics

DOI: 10.1017/9781108588270
First published online: January 2020

Maria Heim
Amherst College, Massachusetts
Author for correspondence: mrheim@amherst.edu

Abstract: "Ethics" was not developed as a separate branch of philosophy in Buddhist traditions until the modern period, though Buddhist philosophers have always been concerned with the moral significance of thoughts, emotions, intentions, actions, virtues, and precepts. Their most penetrating forms of moral reflection have been developed within disciplines of practice aimed at achieving freedom and peace. This Element first offers a brief overview of Buddhist thought and modern scholarly approaches to its diverse forms of moral reflection. It then explores two of the most prominent philosophers from the main strands of the Indian Buddhist tradition – Buddhaghosa and Śāntideva – in a comparative fashion.

Keywords: Buddhism, Buddhaghosa, Śāntideva, compassion

ISBN: 9781108706629 (PB), 9781108588270 (OC)
ISSN: 2516-4031 (online), ISSN 2516-4023 (print)

Contents

1 Introduction

What is good, what is bad? What is blameworthy, what is blameless? What should be practiced, what should not be practiced? What, when done, leads to my lasting harm and suffering, and what, when done, leads to my lasting welfare and happiness?

(Bodhi 2015: 140).

These searching questions recur in several different places in the Buddha's sermons as recorded in some of the earliest scriptures of Buddhism. In one instance, the Buddha enjoins a young man to ask these questions of wise people wherever he may find them to help him discover what is important about action and its effects (Ñāṇamoli and Bodhi 2001: 1057). In another context, this time of a king wondering how to rule justly and well, the king is urged to ask these same questions of his wise advisors (Walshe 1995: 397). In yet another place in the scriptures, the same list of questions had been asked by the Buddha himself during his own long journey toward spiritual awakening (Walshe 1995: 449). In each case, these inquiries into the good and the blameless, on how we should live and what our practices should be, and finally, how to achieve welfare and happiness, can be taken to be the beginnings of Buddhist inquiries into moral philosophy. This Element takes up these questions by close study of the writings of two of Buddhism's most significant moral thinkers, Buddhaghosa and Śāntideva. Both engage in systematic explorations of the Buddha's teachings and how an ideal Buddhist life should be carried out. But they belong to quite different periods and traditions in the intellectual world of ancient India. Buddhaghosa (fifth century CE) was the foremost commentator on the scriptures of the Theravada tradition and wrote a lengthy account of the moral and religious life called the *Path of Purification* that has been highly influential in the Theravada tradition to this day; originally from India, he headed a team of scholars in Sri Lanka. Śāntideva (seventh to eighth century CE) was a Mahayana thinker based at Nālandā University in Bihar and wrote two works that survive, *Training Anthology* and *Guide to the Bodhisattva's Way of Life*, that went on to become highly influential in Tibetan schools of Buddhism. Though their visions overlap in some respects, they differ substantially in both the nature of the moral vision they offer and their styles of moral inquiry into it. By reading them together we can begin to discern something of the complexity and texture of Indian Buddhist thinking about fundamental moral questions of human life.

1.1 Comparative Philosophy and Questions of Approach

Although ordinary English speakers sometimes blur the lines between ethics and morality, it is helpful to distinguish what is meant by these two terms for the sake of philosophical precision and to help us engage in the cross-cultural work of exploring Buddhism with them. One way of defining them would suggest that "morality" concerns precepts, rules, ideals, virtues, practices, and norms about how to live, and if we take "moral philosophy" or "ethical thought" in a general way as reflection on such matters, then it is found everywhere in Buddhist texts. Some usages of "ethics," in contrast, can be taken more narrowly to refer to the branch of philosophy that engages in a certain form of systematic reflection on morality where people stand back from their moral norms and ideas and reflect on why and how they are valued and can be justified. Arguments of justification often entail identifying the sources of morality by advancing arguments about reality or about human nature that result in ethical theories. In Western thought, at least since the time of Plato and Aristotle, one dominant mode of ethical reflection of this sort has taken place in systematic treatises justifying moral principles and ideals through abstract rational argumentation.

There is general consensus in the field of Buddhist studies that Buddhist thinkers did not offer systematic ethical theories justifying moral principles in this way, though their texts everywhere explore moral psychology, exhort moral behavior, posit moral rules and norms, and explore virtue and high moral ideals (Dreyfus 1995; Gowens 2013; Edelglass 2013). This is not because Buddhists did not practice systematic philosophy or were not adept at philosophical argumentation at all, for in the areas of metaphysics, logic, and epistemology we find works analogous to Western philosophy. Rather, in the area of morality their concerns were less abstract and more focused on practical aims of moral and religious training and transformation.

There have been a range of responses to this situation. Some contemporary scholars have attempted to construct what they take to be the implicit or tacit ethical theory underlying Buddhist moral views, a task that has involved identifying which of the three main Western ethical theories – virtue theory, consequentialism, or rule-based deontological principles – best describes Buddhist moral thought. There are those who liken Buddhism to Aristotelian virtue ethics (Keown 1992; Clayton 2006), emphasizing that Buddhists were concerned chiefly with questions of developing character. Others have seen forms of reasoning in certain Buddhist texts that can be helpfully identified as consequentialist and have gone on to argue that Buddhist ethics as a whole puts forward various forms of consequentialism (Goodman 2009). These efforts have spawned an industry of debate on these questions with scholars offering hybrid or qualified versions of these types of arguments (e.g. Vélez de Cea 2004; Harris 2015; Vasen 2018).

These constructive efforts are not without hazards. One is a tendency to treat Buddhism in holistic terms: Since the unstated theory thought to be undergirding "Buddhist" thought is just that, largely unstated in the texts, it need not be tethered closely to particular Buddhist texts or traditions and can thence be generally posited of the tradition, or large swaths of it, rather casually. Because they aim at a very high level of abstraction and generality, such efforts tend to generalize Buddhism to the point of characterizing it with a single ethical theory (revealing "the nature of Buddhist ethics" as founding father of this style of Buddhist ethics, Damien Keown, puts it in the title of his book). This move elides the enormous diversity, heterogeneity, and contestation in moral views and approaches that emerged across Buddhism's 2,500 years of extraordinarily prolific intellectual history spanning most of the continent of Asia (and now beyond it) and across widely divergent schools, traditions, cultures, civilizations, and even scriptural corpuses. In these comparative and constructive efforts, we often lose sight of particular Buddhist thinkers and texts and the debates between them, or, when a particular thinker is showcased as evidence for the general theory, he is pressed into "representing" the whole. Those of us uneasy about this holism point out that certain Buddhist discourses resist general theories of this sort (Hallisey 1996) and may have deliberately abjured this style of abstract theory in favor of more pragmatic or phenomenological approaches. We would also note that no one assumes that 2,500 years of Western philosophy has yielded only one ethical theory; in European thought, particular thinkers and texts are studied with care and precision and an eye for difference and disagreement. Why approach Buddhist intellectual history so differently?

Another hazard is that some of these efforts assume the precedence and universalism of Western theory and take it as axiomatic that non-Western philosophy must be interpreted in its terms. Clayton, for example, asserts that "in order to make sense of Śāntideva's morality, we would have to use a framework" drawn from the West (2009: 15). Too often Western theory is assumed to be the universal form of human thought and non-Western traditions simply offer data to be assimilated to it or rationalized within its frameworks. But I think that one ambition of doing cross-cultural philosophy in the first place is a chance to achieve quite the opposite. That is, when we come to understand how Buddhists deliberated on morality in their own distinctive terms, we may discern markedly different systems that can help provincialize Western theory (by showing how it is not universal) and disrupt its hegemonies (by offering serious alternatives to it). Working closely on Buddhist thinkers by learning how to interpret their own discourses, purposes, and forms of moral thought might suggest different starting places and ways of deliberating about morality that can help us notice and reconsider bedrock assumptions of the modern West.

With these concerns in mind, my study focuses on Buddhaghosa and
Śāntideva to work systematically through their modes of thinking about
how to live and what is good for human beings. While not disavowing
comparison – indeed comparing them to each other is a useful analytic tool
for discerning both patterns and differences – my aim is not to uncover or
construct a single "Buddhist" theory that they share, and still less to frame
their work in Western philosophical terms (though a philosophical vocabulary
and occasional analogues drawn from the West are sometimes useful in an
interpretative project like this). I occasionally suggest comparative forays into
non-Buddhist moral thought ranging from the Stoics to Iris Murdoch as
helpful for sharpening my analysis or generating further questions, but such
forays are always in the service of closer analytic work on Buddhaghosa and
Śāntideva.

Although my focus is trained on the moral visions of these two ancient
Indian thinkers, it might be helpful to the reader unfamiliar with the field to
suggest other types of work being done in Buddhist ethics. One of the most
robust areas is in applied ethics as scholars have looked to Buddhist resources
to consider the ecological crisis, human rights, issues of gender and sexuality,
economic and political philosophy, the ethics of war, end-of-life issues, and
animal rights (see, for example, a recent volume of collected papers edited by
Cozort and Shields 2018; Keown 2005; and some of the essays in Emmanuel
2013). Engaged Buddhism, a modern effort to cast Buddhism as socially and
politically activist, has been well studied in the literature (King 2009; Queen
and King 1996), and readers may also wish to read the Dalai Lama's writings
(e.g. Gyatso 1999), and the works of B. R. Ambedkar, Thich Nhat Hanh,
Pema Chödrön, and Sulak Sivaraksa as prominent examples. Though this
book focuses on the Indian tradition, there is of course important work in East
Asian and Tibetan moral thought that should be considered as well (here also
Cozort and Shields 2018 is useful). Finally, while often neglected in considerations of philosophical ethics, anthropologists bring to the table important insights and methodological considerations about ethics and morality,
some of which will have resonance with themes explored here (e.g. Desjarlais
2003; Eberhardt 2006).

I write with a diverse audience in mind, ranging from students and
scholars new to Buddhism seeking to gain a foothold in its ethical traditions
to more seasoned scholars who may yet find something new and provocative
in these pages. Taking up two of Buddhism's most esteemed thinkers in
comparative fashion can reveal some of the nuances in their approaches
even as it helps the newcomer appreciate some of the complexity in the
tradition.

1.2 The Human Condition

It will be useful at the outset to explicate the starting places that both Buddhaghosa and Śāntideva assume and from which they build their visions of how to live. We turn then to the insights the Buddha had about the human condition that articulate his extraordinary program of human transformation and liberation. In what has often been compared to a medical doctor's diagnosis, the Buddha articulated, in his first sermon, the Four Noble Truths: (1) life is characterized by suffering; (2) this suffering has a cause; (3) suffering can end; and (4) the Noble Eightfold Path can bring about its end.[1]

By suffering what is meant is a range of phenomena from disappointment and frustration to the suffering of old age and illness and the deep sorrow we will face in losing our loved ones and eventually experiencing our own decay and death. Of course, life does not involve *only* suffering and for the fortunate among us there may be many moments of happiness and pleasure. But these are finite and, above all, highly contingent and impossible to secure permanently. The conditions that bring us happiness are difficult to hold on to because our desires and hopes are ever changing and never satisfied. Experience itself is transient, and our youth, health, and loved ones will sooner or later slip away from us. And the conditions of the world in which we live are to a large extent out of our direct control. This sense of the provisional and conditioned nature of even our happiness is itself part of what is meant by "suffering" in this teaching.

This sober assessment of the human condition is fortunately followed by a diagnosis in the Second Truth of what causes this predicament. The Buddha discerned the cause of suffering to be the desire and craving at the heart of human psychology: We want things to be otherwise than what they are and so constantly bump up against the frustration of our wishes. The Third Truth identifies the solution or the end of human suffering, which is the ceasing of the relentless desire that drives us. The end of suffering is the end of desire, and both are "nirvana," the extraordinary and complete freedom from the contingency and suffering otherwise characteristic of human life (nirvana is variously termed "awakening" and "enlightenment" in English sources). Finally, the Fourth Truth is the doctor's prescription to achieve the end of suffering, a series of eight specific practices and reorientations that comprise a "path" to nirvana.

The Eightfold Path is presented as eight sequential items, but though there is a rationality to their ordering, they need not be developed in the order given and, in fact, each supports the others. The first is *right view*, which is understanding

---

[1] These four axioms are given in the Buddha's first sermon. For an accessible translation of this sermon, on which the summary in this section is based, see Bodhi 2015: 75–78 and 239–240.

intellectually and, more importantly, existentially, the Four Noble Truths. The second is *right intention*, which aims at giving up more than one needs, being harmless toward others, and having good will. The next three comprise much of what Buddhists value as morally virtuous verbal and physical actions: *right speech* (avoiding lying, slander, harsh words, and gossip); *right action* (avoiding taking life, stealing, and sexual misconduct); and *right livelihood* (practicing a means of livelihood that does not contravene the other practices of the Eightfold Path). Finally, the last three items involve the transformation of one's awareness and attention at very fundamental levels: *right effort* (restraining and abandoning toxic defilements, and developing and maintaining healthy and good states); *right mindfulness* (learning to attend to body, feeling, mind, and all experiential phenomena), and *right concentration* (developing specific kinds of meditation).

The details of this path – such as what precisely is meant by toxic defilements, healthy and good states, and so on – will be further explained, but for now it is important for the reader to see how this teaching offers an overall framework for assessing the human condition and supplies a series of moral and contemplative practices to radically transform it. These basic teachings are foundational for the visions of human transformation that both Buddhaghosa and Śāntideva develop further. And they present three key premises for how questions of the moral life are framed in the Indian Buddhist tradition and, as a result, how we are to approach them.

First, the moral life is embedded in a spiritual or religious journey. To be sure, the Buddha offered moral advice to ordinary people who may not be on this rigorous spiritual path, and when speaking with kings had much to say on moral norms of statecraft and the outlines of an ideal social order. But the early Indian Buddhist tradition's most sustained philosophical attention and reflection on what we might separate out as "morality" occurred in the context of this soteriological ideal, that is to say, in the service of spiritual liberation. It might be useful to consider the analogue of the Stoic philosophers, and indeed many premodern moral thinkers in the Western tradition, for whom philosophy was a "way of life" rather than merely rational argumentation. Or perhaps in the ancient world, rational argumentation about how to live was always in the service of actually living it in a context of a like-minded community of rule-following practitioners sharing a collective commitment to the dogmas and teleological goals of their tradition (see Hadot 1995). Buddhist thinking about morality occurred within the Eightfold Path's therapeutic practices aimed at alleviating and ultimately eliminating suffering in order to achieve the ultimate freedom from the contingency of human life that is Buddhism's highest ideal, nirvana. Though not limited to the monastic community, these teachings were originally aimed primarily at men and women willing to leave the household life and live as celibate monks and nuns to practice them undistractedly.

Second, the moral life is conceived as a *path*. The vision articulated here and in the work of both Buddhaghosa and Śāntideva is a gradual moral development over time working toward a particular aim. Human life as it stands is inadequate and the moral life is the means to redress it in order to transcend the depredations of suffering and desire. Moral thought is thus not a matter of abstract principles, dilemma-based problems about runaway trolleys, or generating ethical theory as a purely intellectual enterprise. Rather it is always in the service of the pragmatic therapeutic and liberating ambitions of the tradition. Further, though I can only signal the issue here with a promise to come back to it later, the relationship between the path and the goal was a complex one for many Buddhist thinkers, including the two we will be studying. There are hints that the path *is* the goal in certain important respects.

Finally, the entanglement of morality and meditation in the Eightfold Path and the diagnosis of the cause of human suffering in desire and craving indicate the inescapably *psychological* nature of the whole enterprise. To take up the path is to fundamentally transform one's emotional and perceptual orientation or way of being in the world. Moral practice is a prerequisite to meditation practice, and meditation supports moral development. The ancient Indian milieu in which the Buddha was experimenting with fundamentally altering the human condition offered perhaps the most sustained and finely grained contemplative explorations of experience in human history. The Buddha's explorations and the techniques he learned to reconfigure human experience entailed meticulous scrutiny of that experience, and such scrutiny is fundamental to the path, as for example in the forms of attention required by *right mindfulness*. Thus much of our work will be exploring moral psychology and phenomenology as we consider how attention, perception, emotion, intention, and agency work and can be reconfigured.

1.3 Action, Agency, and Freedom

Foundational to the worldview of Indian Buddhism (as well as the other main religions in ancient India, including Hinduism and Jainism) are the ideas of karma and rebirth. These are essential for making sense of the nature of the human condition and the ideal of release from suffering. Karma means, at bottom, action; and actions, or at least morally relevant actions, are understood to have effects both immediate and long term on ourselves and others. This has implications for how we understand the present in two directions: looking backward and looking forward. *Looking backward* one sees the present as shaped by past actions; *looking forward* one sees that the future will be shaped by present actions. The Buddha taught this:

> Student, beings are owners of their actions, heirs of the actions, they originate from their actions, are bound to their actions, have actions as their refuge. It is action that distinguishes beings as inferior and superior (Bodhi 2015: 162).

When he speaks of our being "heir" to our actions, he means that we inherit the effects of actions done in both the recent and remote past: Past actions create and constrain who we are now. When he says that we have actions as our "refuge," he means that we can perform, now, actions that will protect us both now and in the future. In an important sense, one *is* what one *does*. If one performs low, base, and immoral things like stealing, raping, and killing, one is inferior; if one acts harmlessly, honestly, and with good will, one is superior; and both will shape the sort of being one will become.

These ideas about actions were conceived within a widely assumed worldview that included rebirth. That is, this life is not the only one: All of us have been born, lived, and died in countless times in the past. And in the future, we will continue to be reborn unless the cycle is interrupted and brought to an end by the achievement of nirvana. This doctrine has several implications for understanding the Four Noble Truths and karma. First, when the Buddha asserted that life is suffering, it was meant within this much longer trajectory of conditioned existence. If all we faced was a single lifetime, we might consider aging, loss, and death to be unfortunate but well compensated by the joys and triumphs of the rest of what life has to offer. But in the larger framework of endless rebirth (called *samsara*), the sorrows and losses that we will inevitably incur in this life are just the latest in a long stream of unending sorrows and losses as we have been born, loved, lost, gotten sick, grown old, and died in infinite previous lives in the past. And the cycle will continue relentlessly into the future. This is where the Noble Truths get their force: Life is suffering in this endless and perpetual series of ups and downs, gains and losses, births and deaths. The nature of the series is driven by desire for enduring happiness and relief from suffering in this highly conditioned, constantly changing, and unending reality. The Third Noble Truth posits the complete cessation of all suffering – nirvana – pointing to a state of total freedom removed from samsara altogether.

The mechanism of all these rebirths is karma. We are not randomly born into this or that life with this or that body, social location, set of capacities, and so on, but rather attain them according to our deeds. There are two levels of understanding this. The first is that the world works in a just way: If one performs bad actions (traditionally there are ten), one faces the consequences of those actions in hell or a low or inferior birth as an animal, ghost, or unfortunate human. The ten bad actions are killing, stealing, sexual misconduct, lying, malicious speech, harsh speech, gossip, covetousness, ill will, and holding false views (Bodhi 2015: 156–161). Conversely, moral actions (refraining from the ten bad actions) land one in a high human birth or a heavenly world. None of these lasts forever (there is neither eternal damnation nor final resting place in heaven in Buddhism) as the unremitting and conditioned nature of the whole thing churns ever onward. One eventually wears off the karma that resulted in one's just rewards and is plunged into another birth based on additional actions one has accrued.

A second level for understanding this is more psychologically subtle than a tit-for-tat notion of actions and their recompense. In this way of seeing it, actions create who we are as they habituate and shape our dispositions, modes of awareness, and capacities. To become a killer practiced in violence is to coarsen one's awareness, dull one's sensitivity, harden one's heart, and become increasingly angry, callous, and predatory. And the world does not treat such a person well. It thus seems "natural" to Buddhists that such a person is creating a future in this life and the next of being a predatory and violent animal or hell being. Conversely, one given to goodwill and peaceful modes of practice and awareness is creating and habituating a way of being whereby in a future life one will "naturally" become a spiritually advanced human or deity conditioned by the calm and pleasant modes of awareness that one has developed. Human nature in this sense is not fixed or static – we are and we become what we do.

Although some modern Buddhist figures (such as Stephen Batchelor) have questioned or downplayed samsara in their formulations of Buddhism, samsara and karma are foundational for the Buddha, Buddhaghosa, and Śāntideva, and it will be difficult to make sense of their moral and soteriological paths without them. Once again, these ideas have crucial implications for our purposes of figuring out the nature of moral inquiry in this tradition.

It can appear at first that this is a framework for thinking about morality that is centered on action and, therefore, moral attention is trained on establishing what sort of actions create what sort of consequences. Indeed, Buddhism is full of varying lists of moral prescriptions and proscriptions about action, such as avoiding the ten bad actions, practicing right speech, action, livelihood, and taking the five precepts (vowing to avoid taking life, sexual misconduct, lying, stealing, and intoxicants). But the Buddha also repeatedly emphasized intention and the psychological dimensions of action. In a sense we can say that killing and stealing are bad not only because they harm others, ruin one's reputation, corrode social life, and so on (all effects pointed out by the Buddha), but also because they issue from hatred and greed and in turn reinforce and habituate these and other toxic defilements (the main toxic defilements are greed, hatred, and delusion, but there are related afflictions such as delusion, pride, obstinacy, and so on). The Buddha thought that close phenomenological introspection reveals that whatever the nature of their psychic energy or charge, the toxic defilements are themselves forms of suffering and, in so far as they coarsen and cloud one's experience and issue in karmically significant actions, they of course generate further suffering. Moreover, the Buddha considered "mental actions" (thoughts which do not issue in speech or physical action) to be karmically significant as well. A flash of anger is toxic to oneself even if it does not lead to actual harm to others.

Thus, the state of our mental lives is ultimately responsible for our actions. This returns us to issues of psychology and the role of feeling, perception, emotion, attention, and mastery of one's psychological experience in the moral life, and we can begin to see why three items of the Eightfold Path center on attention to one's experience (*right mindfulness*), sustained effort to remove and keep away toxic defilements and to plant and maintain positive experiences in their place (*right effort*), and meditation techniques to help one achieve this (*right concentration*).

A further consideration is necessary before we can move on from action and karma, and that is how Buddhists think about agency and freedom. The picture of human experience emerging in this account indicates that although humans are highly pliable and constantly changing, and although we differ considerably across individuals, our general condition is full of toxic defilements. We have already seen how craving drives our dissatisfaction in samsara and causes suffering. But we are also prone to anger and aversion when our desires are thwarted and when others make incursions upon us or attain what we desire, and we often fall prey to resentment, envy, ill will, covetousness, and all manner of hatred. Further, we are subject to both routine and grotesque delusions about things, not least about the Four Noble Truths themselves, but also about what will make us happy and at peace. Desire and aversion, indeed emotions of all sorts, constrict and distort our vision and perception, fostering delusion that in turn narrows how we might perceive what actions are even possible. In this conception of human experience, agency is often highly restricted: The more we are clouded by our afflictive emotions, distorted modes of perception, and problematic patterns of thinking, the less free we are to act intelligently and well. We are, in fact, profoundly *unfree*. It is not that Buddhists denied freedom, but they considered freedom to be something one gradually achieves to the extent that one succeeds in removing toxic and confining emotional, perceptual, and ideological blinders and constrictions. And, of course, freedom is the *telos* of the entire path as nirvana is the ultimate freedom from desire, suffering, and all toxic defilements.

This means that questions about freedom and agency are not generic in the sense of yielding to abstract arguments about whether or not humans have free will (indeed, the notion of "free will" is a Western construction and has no obvious correlate in Buddhist thought), but rather, that they always concern practical matters centered on moral and religious practice. Freedom is a gradual achievement as one uproots the greed, hatred, or delusion that restrict one's agency and keep one trapped in samsara. Again, we see the logic of the path metaphor of gradual, rigorous, and sustained transformation developed at the levels of both action and psychology.

Finally, these considerations about agency are related to an important teaching deployed in all forms of Buddhism that dissolves the notion of "self" in order to make sense of the changing nature of human experience and the possibilities of radical transformation in it. If the self is a fixed, unchanging entity, then it is hard to make sense of the fluctuations and changes in our experience. Nothing, it is posited, remains stable underneath these fluctuations. In some contexts, as we will see, this teaching may help dismantle the self-ishness and ego at the heart of all of our moral failings, as well as the deepest self-orientation at the root of our most basic distortions in perception and cognition. Here it may be useful to note that we can use the word "self" in several ways, but two are salient here to distinguish: We can use it as the reflexive pronoun (oneself, myself, yourself), and we can refer to "the self" in a metaphysical way that attributes ontological reality to personhood, a soul, an enduring entity. Buddhists freely helped themselves to the first and more quotidian usage without assenting to the latter usage, which involves a claim they usually emphatically deny.

1.4 Contemplative Practices of Purification and Transformation

The final set of preliminary considerations that are helpful before turning in earnest to Buddhaghosa and Śāntideva concerns Buddhist emphases on practices of self-examination, purification, and transformation. Much of what we have observed in the previous two sections foregrounds this topic. We have seen that morality lies intertwined with contemplative practices scrutinizing phenomenological life in a path toward freedom from craving and suffering. And we have seen how moral agency is gradually acquired as one learns how to eliminate the psychological limitations on what we can know about the world and how we can act in it. At the practical level, the situation is to be addressed by removing problematic qualities of experience, whether at the grosser level of harmful actions or at the much more subtle level of harmful thoughts and feelings, and replacing them with actions, thoughts, and emotions that are more capacious, pleasant, and freeing.

Sometimes the Buddha used a simile of agricultural cultivation to indicate how this is to be done. Just as a garden requires lots of weeding to get out the weeds that take over and crowd out the good crop, so too one's experience needs much tending to uproot the weeds (merely pruning or cutting them is not enough) so that the right sorts of dispositions can grow (*Dhammapada*: 337–338; 356–359). Morality is self-cultivation. Sometimes he used a simile of gold, which is dull and hard when full of base metals and other impurities, but becomes shiny, bright, and pliable when these are removed. The gross impurities are the ten bad actions while the more subtle impurities of attachment and aversion take further work to remove (Bodhi 2015: 273). In both similes much of the hard work of the moral life is removal so that one can cultivate desirable moral states.

The Eightfold Path is one important schema in which the Buddha articulated these ideas. Overall it describes practices of identifying and removing the ten bad actions: avoiding lying, slander, harsh words, and gossip (i.e. *right speech*); avoiding taking life, stealing, and sexual misconduct (i.e. *right action*) and stopping thoughts of covetousness, ill will, and wrong view (through *right mindfulness and concentration*). Further, *right effort* is highly systematic about this logic of removing and replacing: restraining existing toxic defilements, and stopping new ones from arising; developing healthy and good states (like mindfulness, peace, equanimity, and insight), and maintaining those that are present.

Although we might say, given its authority in the earliest scriptures, that the Eightfold Path is the paradigmatic articulation of this logic of cultivation and purification as the therapeutic and soteriological path, both Buddhaghosa and Śāntideva developed in systematic ways their own articulations of examining experience, removing problematic actions and experiences, and planting healthy and liberating ones. Buddhaghosa built on the schema of the Eightfold Path to configure it as a threefold schema of the religious life: Morality (*right speech, right action*, and *right livelihood*), Meditation (*right effort, right mindfulness*, and *right contemplation*), and Understanding (*right view* and *right intention*). This threefold schema structures his magnum opus, the *Path of Purification*. Śāntideva's *Training Anthology* begins with giving up all forms of grasping and then structures its contents according to *protecting* one's person, possessions, and welfare; *purifying* one's person, possessions, and welfare; and *cultivating* one's person, possessions, and welfare. In practice these involve removing impurities, keeping at bay the arising of new impurities, and fostering virtuous dispositions (generosity, compassion, forbearance, and so on). His other extant book, *How to Lead an Awakened Life*, describes a journey that unfolds with these very practices. For both thinkers, the moral life involves systematic self-examination, purification, and cultivation.

Meditation programs thus become central to moral thought and development; some of these may be likened to cognitive therapy exercises. It may be helpful to mention an example shared by the two thinkers of a practice that involves "breaking down the barriers" between self and other, as Buddhaghosa puts it, and "exchanging self and other" in Śāntideva. These practices aim at removing hostility, hatred, and indifference toward others, so that one abandons all partiality for oneself. We will consider these extended practices in depth, but I mention them here to suggest the potential for ethical work that introspection and contemplation can involve. Both Buddhaghosa and Śāntideva sequence a series of deliberations, emotional responses, and imaginative interludes one should engage in to dismantle the self-regard that keeps us from identifying with and caring for others. They work tirelessly to root out the resentment, envy, and indifference that prevent one from seeing the other in his or her pain, vulnerability, and complexity. When hatred is removed, lovingkindness and compassion can arise. They note that one's own wishes for happiness and freedom from suffering are experienced by all beings. On what grounds, then, could one privilege one's own concerns? If suffering is bad, Śāntideva asserts, then it is bad for everyone, and should be prevented all around (BCA 8.120). Such therapies of emotion, the nature and extent of which I can only hint at now, reconfigure one's orientation to both self and other, freeing one from egocentrism (and the narcissism, greed, and fear that go along with it) as well as from the anger, hatred, and distortion of others that block one's access to them and hinder one's path to liberation.

Some may find it helpful to reach for analogues in the Western tradition. Iris Murdoch, whose work may usefully be read alongside Buddhist thinking, suggests that "to do philosophy is to explore one's own temperament" as part of the quest for truth (Murdoch 1971: 45), and she also connects morality and the achievement of freedom to expanding attention and vision. Looking to premodern Western thought, scholars of Buddhism have turned in recent decades to the work of Michel Foucault and Pierre Hadot for useful alternatives to analytic philosophy that can provide different lenses through which to view Buddhist programs of ethics and soteriology. Foucault was interested in how disciplinary cultures, which can include institutional forces as well as ideologies, can provide modes of "caring for oneself." He spoke of "technologies of the self" that permit "individuals by their own means or with the help of others a certain number of operations on their own bodies and souls, thoughts, conduct, and way of being, so as to transform themselves in order to attain a certain state of happiness, purity, wisdom, perfection, and immortality" (Foucault 1997: 225). For me, Foucault is especially useful because he draws on the ancient socratic idea that freedom is to be found in self-mastery, and that certain disciplinary regimes and technologies can lead to such freedom. Then he signals the importance of this freedom for ethics. The "very stuff [*matière*] of ethics," he asserts, is the "freedom of the subject and its relationship to others" (Foucault 1997: 300). The gradual achievement of free-dom through disciplinary technologies that examine, purify, and cultivate the person make morality possible.

In somewhat similar ways, but through reading the Stoics, Hadot deploys the language of "spiritual exercises" to indicate ancient Western philosophy's prac-tices of transformation. His focus on dialogues and practices, as well as consider-ing a range of textual genres philosophically (such as Marcus Aurelius' *Meditations*), led him to argue that ancient philosophy was not merely rational argumentation for its own sake but entailed an entire "way of life." For Hadot, "spiritual exercises" were regimens of *askèsis*, that is, practices, trainings, and habituations including study, meditation, modes of dialogue, physical comport-ment, and living within the rules, decorum, and dogmas of one's philosophical school. Spiritual exercises "engage the totality of the spirit," aiming not only at moral progress but at "the transformation of our vision of the world, and the metamorphosis of our being" (Hadot 1995: 127). According to Hadot, the exercises teach one how to live, how to dialogue, how to study, and how to die; one studies, engages the wise in discussion, and practices contemplative medita-tions that deploy attention and imagination. As in Buddhism, moral development is embedded within a larger disciplined quest for truth and realization.

The resources and limitations of these two Western philosophical orientations and their applicability to Buddhist ethics have at this point been well mined in the literature (e.g. Kapstein 2013; Ram-Prasad 2018; Fiordalis 2018). I will not attempt to develop these comparative possibilities further here, preferring instead to stay well within the terms and frameworks that Buddhaghosa and Śāntideva offer. But I appreciate how these thinkers demonstrate that exercises of self-transformation, and the genres that articulate them, constituted an essential and rigorous strand of the Western philosophical tradition, and one that can enrich how we might think about ethics and moral philosophy as we turn to Buddhist philosophical discourse.

2 Buddhaghosa and the Analysis of Moral Experience and Development

We do not have much hard historical evidence about the details of Buddhaghosa's life, but the legends describe him as an intellectual in India who joined a Buddhist monastery in order to learn about the Abhidhamma, a canonical textual tradition analyzing experience. He proved an extraordinarily talented scholar and was sent to Sri Lanka to edit and translate the commentaries on the Pali recension of the early Buddhist scriptures. The commentaries had been preserved in ancient Sinhala, and he was to translate them into the cosmopolitan language of Pali (a language closely related to Sanskrit). Arriving in Sri Lanka, he composed his *Path of Purification (Visuddhimagga)*, a nearly 750-page articulation of the Buddhist path, to prove his mettle to the monastic authorities there. He was granted permission to produce the commentaries, likely as the head of a team of scholars (given the magnitude of the project and sheer size of the final achievement). His work represents, after the Buddha's scriptures themselves, the most prolific and systematic formulation of the teachings that comprise the early Pali Theravada intellectual tradition.

Although Theravada is the name of his school as we refer to it today, Buddhaghosa would have taken himself to be working within the Mahāvihāra, the Great Monastery, and he identified himself as an Analyst (Vibhajjavādin), which may have been a sectarian identifier but also signaled for him a style of intellectual work. The Analyst, he says, "does not misrepresent the teachers, does not launch into his own view, does not quarrel with the views of others, does not deviate from the Sutta [that is, the Buddha's sermons], stays in accordance with the Vinaya [the monastic rules], considers the great authorities, illuminates the Teaching, takes up the meaning and then returns again to that meaning by explaining it with different methods" (Vism XVII.25 and *Sammohavinodanī* 130 [my translation]).[2] Buddhaghosa takes himself to be drawing out what is said in the scriptures and then providing many modes of analysis and methods for interpreting and explaining them. He does not claim to offer metaphysical arguments about reality or to engage in epistemological reasoning or debate about how we know reality, much in contrast to his contemporaries in India who did both.

In some ways, then, Buddhaghosa's vision is a very conservative version of scholarly practice that involves exegetical development of the scriptures (which, of course, was his task as an editor and translator of the commentaries and how he understood what he was doing in the *Path of Purification*); his project is largely hermeneutic. At the same time, his "returning again to the meaning and explaining it with different methods" turns out to be a rather

---

[2] The *Path of Purification* (*Visuddhimagga*, abbreviated here as Vism) is translated by Ñāṇamoli 1991, and I rely, unless otherwise noted (as here), on his translations, cited by paragraph. The *Sammohavinodanī* is translated by Ñāṇamoli 1996. For those new to Buddhism, Gethin 1998 is an accessible historical introduction to Buddhism with an emphasis on the Indian foundations; Bodhi 2015 is a useful selection of Pali Buddhist scriptures.

modest way of describing an extraordinarily fecund practice of analytically developing ideas and practices. The *Path of Purification* analyzes experience with the aim of transforming it through the Buddha's many teachings on Morality, Concentration, and Understanding. It is a guidebook for celibate monastics who were already committed to its religious path; it was not written to be a free-standing philosophical argument about morality or ethics treated in the abstract. Throughout, Buddhaghosa is engaged in phenomenological and contemplative analysis rather than metaphysical assertion or argument.[3] In other words, he does not ground his practical and phenomenological work by arguing for an ontology either of reality or of experience. This is not to deny that he was committed to the truths and dogmas of his school (which he presumed rather than argued for), but rather to describe the nature of his project and what he claims to be doing. Throughout his oeuvre, we see analyses of many different sorts that examine and reexamine experience, always within the terms of Buddhist doctrine and for the pragmatic purposes of the overall therapeutic and soteriological aims of the path.

These considerations have entailments for how we read him. Although his efforts are focused on a therapeutic path for a confirmed (or at least ideal) audience of religious practitioners committed to examining and transforming their experience through this discipline, and we have to understand it within these terms, we may still discern a moral phenomenology, and style of inquiry into it, instructive for other contexts. Recently, philosophers have taken up Buddhaghosa's treatment of experience and considered it in light of contemporary philosophical questions. Jonardon Ganeri notes the "unparalleled brilliance" in Buddhaghosa's thinking about attention for how it can contribute to philosophy of mind, consciousness, and ethics (Ganeri 2017: 31). We might say, though, that Ganeri's project of bringing Buddhaghosa's thinking into contemporary epistemological, metaphysical, and ethical discussions is largely a constructive one, based on ideas inspired, though not developed in these particular ways, by Buddhaghosa. Chakravarthi Ram-Prasad has found in Buddhaghosa a phenomenological method worth putting into conversation with the Western phenomenological tradition, specifically Merleau-Ponty, on bodily subjectivity and the "ecology of experience" in ways that counter and offer fresh alternatives to both Cartesian dualist and reductive physicalist readings of the human being (Ram-Prasad 2018).

For our purposes, reading Buddhaghosa with an eye to morality and ethics requires us first to grasp how analyzing experience can be a moral concern,

---

[3] For more work discussing the nature of Buddhaghosa's phenomenological method, see Ram-Prasad 2018, chapter 3; Heim and Ram-Prasad 2018; and Heim 2018, especially chapter 4.

and second, to see how his strategies for analyzing and changing experience are a form of moral philosophy. What does examining experience teach us about action, feeling, intention, motivation, and agency? What are the moral sentiments that conduce to moral action and transformation? What are the toxic defilements that hinder moral progress? Can we speak of moral perception or capacities for attention that help or inhibit moral agency? And, most importantly, how can humans change? How do we identify and reconfigure our most deeply rooted habits of thought, perception, and emotion in ways that make us happier and more free? Such questions are the domain of moral psychology and moral phenomenology, and much Buddhist thought contributes to this area of scholarly reflection (see also Garfield 2010; McRae 2018).

As mentioned earlier, the *Path of Purification* is a carefully structured disciplinary path beginning with a chapter on Morality, followed by a section on specific Concentration practices, and ending in a section on Understanding. My treatment of Buddhaghosa will show how he treats each of these in detail through his distinctive analytical methods. A brief précis of these three can indicate what is to come.

Morality or, more precisely, moral precepts (*sīla*) in which one abstains from the ten bad actions, is the foundation or starting place of the path because it offers stability for clear vision, contemplation, and advancing toward understanding (Vism I.11). Buddhaghosa's first chapter is dedicated to morality. Only when one is established, at least to some degree, in the precepts, can one do the deeper contemplative work required for transformation (and then further work on contemplation and understanding will reinforce further work on morality). An immoral person given to killing, lying, and stealing, for example is, in practice, too troubled (if not by bad conscience then by the authorities and others) to achieve the level of concentration needed to advance on the path. These grosser actions need to be reined in first.

Concentration (*samādhi*) – the meditation practices that comprise the middle section of the *Path of Purification* – is built on the foundation of morality. These are specific exercises for calming and focusing the mind aimed at concrete therapeutic work to be done by a monk working with a teacher on his spiritual progress (the entire treatise is written with monastics in mind, and I use the male pronoun advisedly – though the practices and goal are not limited to men, Buddhaghosa is largely assuming and writing for a male subject). Some are exercises of purifying oneself of hatred; others dismantle lust and desire, others take on death, and others orient the practitioner to a high moral ideal. They are all quite complex, intricate, and challenging, for it is here that the very difficult and subtle work of fundamentally reconstituting experience gets tackled.

Morality and Concentration together conduce to Understanding (*paññā*). Understanding (often translated as "wisdom") is defined as a process or activity by Buddhaghosa – the *act* of understanding (Vism XIV.3) – and so should not be seen as a final state of knowledge so much as a continual practice of "knowing and seeing" (*ñāṇadassana*). The kind of achievement of understanding meant at this stage in the path is a mode of perceiving and attending that pervades all moments of perception and awareness, and knows these and the other phenomena of experiential life as such. This kind of understanding is said to be liberating; indeed, it *is* liberation (nirvana) because by discerning the nature of the phenomena of awareness disentangled from the perceptual, emotional, cognitive, and ideological overlay that normally clouds and distorts one's experience, one can be liberated from them.

2.1 Morality

Morality (*sīla*) in general is the abstaining from the ten bad actions: not killing, not stealing, not committing sexual misconduct, not lying, not using malicious speech, not using harsh speech, not gossiping, not being covetous, not having ill will, and not holding or promoting false views – these are, in fact, the "ten good actions" (Vism I.17). It is notable that morality in the *Path of Purification* is not described in particularly proactive terms as cultivating particular virtues, performing concrete duties, or developing a certain kind of character. Nor is it treated abstractly; these ten moral actions are a concrete matter of stopping and refraining from specific mental, verbal, and physical actions. Morality is situated at the start of the religious path for the monastic practitioner because, when one abstains from these actions, one purifies the grosser aspects of conduct and makes it possible to then do further work purifying emotions, forms of perception, and habitual tendencies in the Concentration and Understanding exercises.

Buddhaghosa practiced a method of systematic intellectual work that comes to an object of experience from many sides and considers it under many different aspects; the anti-essentialist thrust of his thinking resists single definitions and reductionist lines of inquiry. When taking up a topic, he begins with an outline or "matrix" (*mātikā*) that lists various further questions and topics that can cast different kinds of light on it. A matrix is a list that generates further lists, exegesis, and analytical practice. This methodology of scaffolding a wide range of different kinds of questions and lines of inquiry into a phenomenon allows for great precision as well as practices of reconsidering a phenomenon from diverse aspects and modes. It is a kind of modal analytical practice that is also, as we will come to see, used in his contemplative exercises, and it constitutes a fundamental practice of the wisdom or understanding that is the *telos* of the entire path.

About morality, he says in his opening chapter of the *Path of Purification*, we should first ask this matrix of questions:

> (1) *what is morality?* (2) *what is its characteristic feature?* (3) *what is its function?* (4) *how does it manifest?* (5) *what are its proximate causes?* (6) *what are its benefits?* (7) *what kinds of morality are there?* (8) *what are its defilements?* (9) *what is moral purification?* (Vism I.16)

He then proceeds, in detail and expansively, to answer one-by-one each of these questions, often with further lists and further questions, to explore how morality can be taken up for analysis under each of these topics. These nine questions can structure our treatment of his thinking on morality, although our treatment is by necessity only a brief account of what he treats in detail.

We can begin to demonstrate how his style of analysis works as we engage the first of this string of questions: (1) *what is morality?* Morality (*sīla*), he says, is fourfold and can begin to be analyzed in these different ways.

(1) *What is Morality?*

    (1.a) morality as intention (*cetanā*)
    (1.b) morality as mental phenomena (*cetasika*)
    (1.c) morality as restraint (*saṃvara*)
    (1.d) morality as nontransgression (*avītikkama*) (Vism I.16)

The first two deal with what we would consider aspects of the psychological dimensions of morality. Starting with (1.a), morality can be conceived as moral *intention*, where there are various types of moral intention, and specifically, seven are listed: the moral intention when one refrains from killing, the moral intention one has when one refrains from stealing, the moral intention one has when one refrains from committing sexual misconduct, from harsh speech, from malicious speech, from lying, and from gossip. In other words, there are different kinds of intentions involved when one is abstaining from the first seven of the ten immoral actions.

The word "intention" does not mean a moral choice, decision, or the will, but rather an agentive capacity happening at a more rudimentary level of the psychological processes of "constructing" or fashioning the object of one's experience and activity; in this it is more like the modern philosophical idea of "intentionality" as the "aboutness" of the object of experience, with a great deal of interest in the constructive nature of that aboutness (see Heim 2014). At the same time, this interest in how the flow of experience gets put together is not discussed in terms of epistemological arguments about the veracity of our representations or their correspondence to objects "out there"; rather, intention concerns the fashioning of the objects of experience out of the other phenomena of awareness. When one refrains from killing, there is an intentionality – that is, a construction of experience itself out of and through which what one perceives, attends to, senses, feels, and so on – that precludes an act of killing. This construction is conditioned by what else is present in one's psychology in that moment of experience, but it is not entirely determined by it, and it is in this constructive activity that an important element of agency is located. We begin to see that morality is a complex set of operations occurring through how we put together our experience of the world with the resources of our psychological lives. Agency occurs at a deeper level or prior activity than the moment of choice: By the time one makes a decision to act, much has gone on prior to it to shape how one perceives and frames the choice. It is this very prior activity that is referred to as "intention" in this tradition.

Additionally, morality can also be conceived as (1.b) other *mental or psychological phenomena*; this refers to additional psychological factors that preclude immoral action. Three are listed: the presence of the mental phenomenon of "non-covetousness" (which pushes out greed and thus prevents immoral actions like stealing), of non-ill will (a lovingkindness that, when present, makes hatred and violence impossible at that moment), and of right view (avoiding the distortions of view that produce immoral action) (Vism I.17). These cover the last three of the ten moral actions, which are mental rather than physical or verbal actions. The formulations of these in negative terms ("non-covetousness") are helpfully understood if we recall the gardening metaphor: Removing the weeds of covetousness (a strong form of greed that longs for others' things), ill will (a strong form of hatred in that one does not merely despise the other, but wishes harm to come to them), and wrong view (a strong fortification of delusion) is the psychological work of morality because moral actions cannot happen at all as long as these are present.

Morality can also be conceived as a type of (1.c) *restraint*, the active holding oneself back from violating moral norms. Buddhaghosa lists five types of restraint: restraint by monastic precepts, restraint by exertion, restraint by forbearance, restraint by knowledge, and restraint by mindfulness practice (where attending to one's phenomenological states can also help one restrain oneself, as when simply becoming aware of one's greed can often help one to curb it) (Vism I.18). In this conception, morality can be conceived variously as a matter of external rules, knowledge, the virtue of forbearance (which checks anger and hate), or exercising exertion or self-awareness that can also provide sites of agency to curb wrongdoing.

Finally, we can see that at one level morality can also be defined as simply (1. d) *nontransgression*, not doing immoral things (that is, avoiding the ten immoral actions of killing, stealing, sexual misconduct, lying, malicious speech, harsh speech, gossip, covetousness, ill will, and holding wrong views). At one level, morality comes down to a matter of transgression or nontransgression; here, it is simply the *not doing* of actions that are immoral. Again, we may be struck by the way this conception of morality is more a matter of *not doing* blameworthy actions than committing positive, virtuous actions. This is because virtues, such as generosity (*dāna*) or compassion (*karuṇā*), tend to be treated as specific and distinctive categories in their own rights and are discussed elsewhere; they are not part of *sīla* as such.

We can press on with Buddhaghosa's main matrix of questions: (2–5) *what is morality's characteristic feature, function, manifestation, and proximate causes?* Its *characteristic feature* is "composing" because what is clear in all of the "various ways of analyzing it" is that morality involves coordinating and upholding certain mental states and actions in a consistent way (Vism I.19–20). Its *function* refers to the work of stopping immoral action when immoral action presents itself as an opportunity, and when this function is successful, one is seen as blameless. *What is its manifestation?* It is manifest, or shows up in experience, when impurities are removed (recall the simile of gold and the importance of purification to the whole project). Finally, like all things, morality is conditioned: Causes and conditions both near and remote make it possible. Buddhaghosa is always interested in the nexus of causes and conditions prompting any phenomenon, and here we see that the analysis of moral experience requires an understanding of what immediately undergirds it. He identifies the *proximate causes* of morality in two moral sentiments, shame (*hiri*) and apprehension (*ottappa*) (Vism I.12–13). These are morally valuable phenomena of fearing one's own and others' approbation if one were to do something wrong (shame) and the fear of the consequences of the deed itself (moral apprehension). These checks on our wrongdoing are not identical with a Christian notion of conscience, but they bear some affinities to it and are much esteemed for how they keep us from harming the world (and so they are called "world-protectors"). Immoral action requires overriding them, and there are exercises in which one can fortify them to keep this from occurring.

Further, (6) *what are the benefits of morality?* According to Buddhaghosa, first and foremost, morality keeps remorse at bay, and remorse is a scratchy, painful affliction. (Of course, this consideration is unlikely to be of use for wrongdoers impervious to remorse, but Buddhaghosa does not consider this possibility as he is assuming an audience of committed Buddhists.) There are further benefits. For the householder, morality also pays off by increasing one's wealth, reputation, and respect in the community; when it comes time to die, one can do so with an easy mind, and one will achieve a happy rebirth. And for householders and monastics alike, prudential considerations further reveal that the virtuous person is well liked, beautiful, esteemed, free of anxiety and self-blame, and happy (Vism I.23–24). The idea that the virtuous are beautiful stems from the idea that anger, hatred, and greed distort the face and make one ugly and unattractive to others, and is a prevalent theme in Buddhist thought (Mrozik 2007: 66–68). Buddhaghosa may be overly optimistic here as hard experience sometimes suggests that the virtuous are not so handsomely rewarded. Nor does he entertain the possibility that people can face moral dilemmas and be required to make hard choices that may be deleterious to their social standing and interests. In his conception (which is assumed rather than argued for), refraining from the ten wrong actions will, in a seamless and straightforward way, yield only benefits.

What are the (7) kinds of morality? There are many kinds of morality because one can analyze it variously and make distinctions for different purposes, and I touch here only on a few of them. For example, one can see morality as both *keeping* and *avoiding*: One keeps or preserves the moral precepts by doing what should be done through faith and energy, and one avoids violating them by staying clear of wrongdoing through faith and mindfulness (mindfulness will help identify problematic states of mind that could lead to wrongdoing) (Vism I.25–26). Another distinction one can make about the kinds of morality is that morality may be both "worldly" and "transcendent," where worldly morality is that motivated by and conducive to the benefits that morality brings to one's life and rebirth, and transcendent morality is that which conduces to one's ultimate freedom (Vism I.25–32). Another distinction is the moralities of monks, nuns, novices, and laypeople, where Buddhaghosa recognizes differences in precepts, standards, and norms for these classes of people. Morality is also gendered for monks and nuns in that they have different monastic codes (nuns have more rules to follow with more stringent standards and higher penalties for infractions), and it differs according to monastic or lay status, with laypeople taking many fewer precepts than monastics (Vism I.25; I.40).

Further, (8) *What are the defilements of morality?* Morality can get "torn" by defilement (*kilesa*), such as when a monk commits a monastic infraction of sexual contact with women (here is one example where we see that Buddhaghosa defaults to assuming a male monastic subject). One should instead endeavor to stay "untorn," like a whole piece of cloth, although amends can be made to purify and restore morality in such cases (Vism I.143). The toxic defilements are ten: greed/lust, hatred, delusion, pride, wrong view, doubt, obstinacy, worry, shamelessness, and lack of moral apprehension (Vism XXII.49). Defining morality in terms of defilement suggests that at least part of what is wrong with sexual misconduct and other moral transgressions is the depraved psychology involved in them. A related term is the "oozing" (*āsava*) that occurs when the toxic defilements issue forth in committing an immoral action. (A frequently encountered synonym for one who has attained nirvana is "one who has eliminated the oozings" [*khīṇāsava*].) A person who has allowed his virtue to be seriously defiled (particularly a monk who has transgressed the precepts on sex) becomes displeasing to others, someone "as unfit to live with as a dead carcass" and as "hard to purify as a cesspit many years old" (Vism I.153–157).

Finally, (8) *what is moral purification?* When things go wrong how does one come clean? To cleanse or begin to purify himself, the reprobate should be subjected to the Buddha's hellfire sermons and implored to change his ways with vivid instruction on the dangers of immorality and the benefits of morality. Technical analysis gives way to moral exhortation in this section of the chapter where monks are informed of the fiery tortures awaiting them in hell for monastic infractions described in lurid detail and in marked contrast to the beautiful composure of immaculate virtue when one's moral conduct is pure (Vism I.143–160). Buddhaghosa ends his chapter on Morality here because he has set the reader up for the deeper psychological exercises described in the section on Concentration that will do this very work of purification.

As we have surveyed this section on Morality, readers have seen how Buddhaghosa's methods of definition work to scaffold different aspects of the phenomenon of morality and then drill down into their workings. Buddhaghosa does not want to settle on a single definition or characterization of morality, because, like all other phenomena, it is multidimensional and admits of various modes of description and consideration. It is also notable what this analysis does not include. Specifically, it lacks an applied ethics arguing for an interpretation of the ten bad actions (*How is sexual misconduct actually defined? Are there ever cases in which killing or lying may be sanctioned? What does malicious or harsh speech actually mean?* And so on.) This is because the fuller definitions of these ten deeds can be found in scripture and Buddhaghosa's commentaries on them elsewhere.[4]

---

[4] For the scriptural account, see Bhikkhu Ñāṇamoli and Bhikkhu Bodhi, trans. *The Middle-Length Discourses of the Buddha: A Translation of the Majjhima Nikāya* 1995: 914–918. Buddhaghosa's commentary on the ten bad actions can be found in Bhikkhu Ñāṇamoli and Bhikkhu Bodhi, trans. *The Discourse on Right View: The Sammādiṭṭhi Sutta and its Commentary* 1991: 26–39 and Pe Maung Tin, trans. *The Expositor* 1999: 128–134. See also Heim 2014: 65–76, which draws from these and other passages on the ten bad and ten good actions.

2.2 Concentration

If the first chapter on Morality addresses the grosser forms of bad action, then the meditation practices in the Concentration section continue the disciplinary project of purifying problematic experience at a deeper level, a purification thought to lead to greater degrees of moral agency. To be sure, stopping grosser forms of immoral action is the prerequisite for advanced meditation exercises (because bad actions mire one in practical difficulties and leave toxic residue in the mind), but the meditation exercises will in turn support the stopping of bad actions and will go further to root out even traces of the defilements that remain. This project involves the removal of problematic emotions and the distortions in perception, modes of attention, and habitual patterns of thinking that stymie agency. This idea is premised on the view that, prior to facing moral choices and dilemmas, what one has permitted oneself to see and feel shapes whether and how one discerns those moral choices to begin with. If the psychological phenomena "underneath" rational and prudential deliberation on the one side, or virtue and character development on the other, are not addressed, then, in the Buddhist view, one's capacities for both of these forms of moral agency are highly constricted. In other words, moral agency is gradually acquired and then only to the extent to which one removes problematic and distorted forms of perception, feeling, attention, and habits of thought present in one's moment-by-moment experience.

Several phenomena are constantly at work in the construction of experience: sensory contact, feeling, perceptual judgement, intention (as the agentive constructive activity we saw earlier), awareness, and attention.[5] How we feel, perceive, intend, and even what we become aware of or attend to in the first place are all inflected by the phenomena that occur in our psychologically encumbered experience. Feeling (*vedanā*) factors highly in moral agency, as we find ourselves buffeted by pleasurable and painful experiences that stoke the desire and aversion that drive so much of what we do; Buddhists see agency and freedom in large measure as enslaved to them, even in our ordinary experience. When consumed with greed for a new house or car, for example, I shape my life and decisions around this aim, often constricting my freedom to seek other pursuits or to find happiness in the things I have. When blinded by anger or revenge, I am held captive to them, tethered to a painful past and fantasies of vengeance that prolong my preoccupation. (Buddhaghosa does not share, for

---

[5] In the Abhidhamma listings that describe phenomena present in every moment of awareness, sensory contact (*phassa*), feeling (*vedanā*), perceptual judgment (*saññā*), intention (*cetanā*), and awareness (*citta*) are present in all moments; Buddhaghosa adds attention (*manasikāra*). See Heim 2014: 92–100.

better or for ill, a notion of social justice activism that draws on anger about injustice; anger has no emancipatory value in his thought.)

Perceptual judgement (*saññā*), as another example about how we construct experience, is the activity that notices and puts a label on a feature of experience, as, for example, when we look up and see a mass of blue and think "blue" or "sky." Even this rudimentary operation varies per person in a myriad of ways. Buddhaghosa gives the example of the skilled carpenter who, with his specialized knowledge, will note and mentally label each of his particular pieces of wood quite differently than those of us who might see just a pile of planks (*Atthasālinī* 110). These considerations make even very basic perceptive and cognitive tasks matters of moral concern as, for example, we consider if and how people notice and perceive suffering and injustice, which are prior but necessary operations to effective moral action and intervention. Attention (*manasikāra*) can also be considered a morally relevant process as when, for example, Buddhaghosa defines love and compassion as specific kinds of "attention to beings," involving first careful looking and seeing others in their particular conditions before one can long for and work toward their welfare.[6]

In these ways the psychological operations of moment-by-moment experience must be addressed – and fundamentally changed – as an essential part of the moral project. Feelings and, more broadly, emotions, are to be radically reconfigured by the purification exercises in the long section in the *Path of Purification* called Concentration. It may be helpful to suggest that Buddhists, along with other thinkers in ancient India, thought that emotions are quite malleable and that with training the problematic ones can be changed or removed, and salutary feelings can be cultivated. Moral development requires attention to both our moment-by-moment reactivity and long-term dispositions through disciplinary training, and we can even learn to be rid of problematic and painful experiences altogether (indeed, that is what liberation is!). In this sense, philosophy can be, as Emily McRae puts it, a "therapy of emotions" (McRae 2015:103; for "philosophy as therapeia," see also Nussbaum 1994; Ganeri and Carlisle 2010).

It is also important to consider the tractability of perception. Beginning with the Buddha himself, Buddhists rejected a naïve realism in our perception of the world. What we perceive is not simply and immediately what is "out there" but rather what gets filtered through the complex psychological apparatus that we bring to each moment of experience. Though Buddhaghosa did not take up in any systematic way epistemological questions regarding what we can know and

---

[6] Pe Maung Tin 1999: 262; see Heim 2017: 183. Ganeri builds on Buddhaghosa's work on attention to develop an ethic of empathy and social cognition (2017, ch. 13). The ethical importance of attention has long been understood by Iris Murdoch (1971: 64).

how we know it, focused as he was on the pragmatic and programmatic phenomenology of transformation, he was ever interested in how humans construct experience. Concentration exercises work at these levels of feeling, perception, attention, and various sentiments and dispositions because these put together our experience. The practices of concentration, called serenity or calming meditations, are exercises that develop or "bring into being" (*bhāvanā*) therapeutic states and activities, such as heightened capacities for attention, greater development of love, compassion, and sympathy, increased pliability and moral sensibility, and so on. We have the space to consider just a few of the most prominent among them, looking particularly at those that cultivate virtues and moral states.

According to Buddhaghosa, one embarks on concentration exercises under the tutelage of a trusted and wise teacher, one who knows one better than one knows oneself. (Given the level of trust required here and the importance of a good teacher, Buddhaghosa gives special attention to how such teachers are to be found and their qualifications at Vism III.61–65). A wise and benevolent teacher is necessary because we need "the voice of another"; given our fundamental weaknesses in habit and disposition, and our thick delusions about what we truly need, left on our own we too often avoid seeing our deepest moral flaws and skirt the most difficult moral tasks. Based on the teacher's evaluation of one's temperament – for everyone is different and exercises are tailored and encouraged based on what kind of work one needs to do – the teacher will recommend a series of exercises (Vism III.61–94). Often at the beginning of one's practice, one finds that the mind skitters around so much that basic and focused attention on a single object is required to get it under control. And so a practice of focusing on a single color or shape for hours daily for several weeks is carefully mapped out. Other exercises counter lust, attachment to the body, and fear of death, such as the corpse meditations of sitting in cremation grounds studying the decay of various kinds of rotting bodies. These extreme practices with corpses are to be carried out only under a carefully monitored disciplinary regime, and only for those battling deep-seated lust and attachment.

For certain other temperaments and problematic dispositions, what is needed is to promote feelings of admiration, moral possibility, and awe by "recollections on the Buddha." These attend in a multifaceted way to the extraordinary moral ideal of the Buddha, allowing the practitioner to see, and to some extent aspire to, his "perfections." The Buddha was said to have achieved thirty perfections of character during his nearly countless previous lives as he prepared to attain nirvana. Ten in particular are extolled in the Theravada: generosity, morality (*sīla*), renunciation, understanding, energy, forbearance, truth, determination, lovingkindness, and equanimity (Vism IX.124). All of these are virtues to be cultivated by the practitioner, although in the Theravada there is no expectation that most people can achieve them to the degree of perfection that the Buddha did; the aim of the soteriological path is to become a liberated person – an *arhat* – not a buddha. (A buddha is a morally perfect being whose nirvana entails discovering and disseminating Buddhist teachings when they are forgotten in the world; an *arhat* is one who has benefited from a buddha's teachings and attained nirvana). Still, the value of knowing and upholding a model of moral perfection itself is thought to be morally beneficial (Vism IX.124). Iris Murdoch also speaks of "magnetic pull of the idea of perfection," where it can work "within a field of study, producing an increasing sense of direction" in moral development (Murdoch 1971: 41, 60).

Some of the most important exercises from the standpoint of developing moral sensibility and agency are the "sublime abidings." Also called the "immeasurables," these four practices can be considered varieties of loving attention: lovingkindness, compassion, sympathetic joy, and equanimity. They are "sublime abidings" because they are the ways of living that deities inhabiting the heavens practice, and they are "immeasurables" because the practice of them never ceases as one extends the love one has for others, both in scope (there are always more beings one can come to love more) and in habit (one's habits and dispositions of love can always admit of further expansion and refinement). Buddhaghosa's exercises for their development yield a complex phenomenology of love and care, and warrant our attention for the moral feeling and perception they develop (see Heim 2017 for an extensive treatment).

First, some definitions. All four are modes of attention that involve very specific types of content: lovingkindness (*mettā*) is wishing for the happiness of others; compassion (*karuṇā*) is longing for those suffering to be free of pain; sympathetic joy (*muditā*) is sharing emotionally in the good fortune and happiness of others; and equanimity (*upekkhā*) is a feeling of peaceful impartiality and balance as one considers others. Buddhaghosa illustrates the differences by his analogy of a mother with four sons: a baby, a sick child, a youth, and a grown man. For the baby she feels lovingkindness, longing for him to thrive; toward the sick child she feels compassion, working for him to get well; toward the youth in the prime of life, she shares in his happiness; and toward her grown-up son she enjoys the calm composure of standing back from fretting over each of his affairs and choices, while still looking on with a loving gaze.[7] This analogy has the virtue of drawing on universally recognizable experiences – what could

---

[7] Vism IX.108. Equanimity is to be done only after having advanced with the first three practices, and so the foundations of lovingkindness, compassion, and sympathetic joy never go away even as one becomes more impartial and balanced in their application. The mother continues to love her grown son.

be more ordinary and yet more powerful than a mother's love for her children? – even while going on to show that they can be subject to further cultivation and expansion. Buddhaghosa's chapter on the sublime abidings provides concrete exercises that develop their intensity and scope, so that one can come to feel intensely these experiences toward all beings.

But why would one want to expand them, especially because the work he describes can be arduous as one tries to arouse them for people who have committed wrongs and injustices or been outright hostile? Resentment, anger, envy, and indifference turn out to be very difficult to dislodge, as evidenced by the hard work the meditator must engage in to eliminate them. Buddhaghosa does not advance ethical arguments about why these are good states; he does not exhort the reader to practice them for the sake of others or on the basis of any sort of moral principle that requires us to become virtuous; they are not moral demands. Moreover, the abidings do not represent all types of love: Some types of love, such as those holding couples and families together, necessarily involve partiality, and Buddhaghosa says nothing about them, addressing his practices to celibate monks who are (at least in theory) removed from such bonds. Rather, the reason one engages in these four specific kinds of love is because they yield freedom for the practitioner. That is, without the rigorous work of lovingkind-ness one remains "slave to the defilements," the anger, envy, resentment, callous indifference, and so on that block freedom and agency (Vism IX.36). These are afflictive and painful emotions that narrow one's vision and restrict our agency, and thus are to be systematically removed so that one can see further and more justly as one works to achieve what he calls the "freedom of the loving heart."[8] Love and compassion are the "antitoxins" that remove the defilements that restrict agency and freedom.

And so one engages in the difficult task of "breaking down barriers" between self, loved ones, neutrals, and then enemies. Ultimately one seeks to break down all barriers between self and other, to the point that if a band of brigands were to seize the practitioner and three others (a dear one, a neutral, and an enemy) and demand one of the four as the price of letting the others go, one would not be able to hand over any of the four (Vism IX.41). (This stands in marked contrast to Śāntideva's verses, which we will consider shortly, that extol dramatic self-sacrifice). In Buddhaghosa's thinking, there is a leveling of love and compas-sion that does not deny love for oneself. In fact, the practices begin with a healthy regard for oneself from which one cultivates lovingkindness outward toward others in an ever-expanding radius. One considers, "I am happy. Just as I want to be happy and dread pain, as I want to live and not to die, so do other

---

[8] Vism IX.9. "Freedom of the loving heart" is my translation of *mettā cetovimutti*.

beings, too" (Vism IX.10). On the basis of the shared hope to be happy and to avoid misery, one becomes committed to other beings. This work of gradually pervading others with love becomes a matter of "identifying oneself with all," to achieve a "sameness with self, without making the distinction 'this is another being,' and so taking beings divided into low, average, or prominent, friendly, hostile, or neutral, and so on, as oneself" (*Sammohavinodanī* 377, my translation). Although Buddhaghosa does not expand this notion of sameness and equality in the direction of arguing for social justice (which many might take to be a major deficiency of his thought and, for that matter, that of other premodern Buddhist thinkers, too), this idea about sameness could become a resource for further constructive work to advance the tradition beyond personal development to broader social, economic, and political ethics (as Garfield 2002 has ably done with Mahayana thought in the cases of human rights and democracy).

Breaking down barriers is done by systematically dismantling the opposites or "enemies" of each of the kinds of love. Anger and resentment block lovingkindness, for example, and so one must cultivate antidotes to them so that lovingkindness can emerge. Love is, in an important sense, the hard work of removing hate. The enemies of compassion are cruelty and indifference, the enemy of sympathetic joy is envy, and the enemies of equanimity are indifference on the one side, and falling back into attraction or aversion on the other, and so losing balance. Buddhaghosa spends much of his time on the first sublime abiding, lovingkindness, because it involves removing all varieties and degrees of resentment, hatred, and anger. The more one does to look inward and cultivate lovingkindness, the more one realizes just how much these basic feelings of aversion are operative in even the subtlest recesses of our psychology, and how much they shape our decisions and actions when left unaddressed.

We can touch only briefly on the main techniques he uses to dispel resentment. First, he recommends that the meditator recall the Buddha's words urging the abandonment of hate and insisting that even if bad men were to seize one and saw off one's limbs, "one who entertained hate in his heart on that account would not be one who carried out my teaching." And the Buddha is cited as asserting that "to repay angry men in kind is worse than to be angry first" (Vism IX.15). These uncompromising teachings show just how toxic and afflictive anger, hatred, and resentment are for the Buddhist path, and how urgent is the imperative to remove them. So one should begin by generating the feeling of lovingkindness for oneself, wishing, "may I be happy!" From there, one lets the same feeling flow outward to one's loved ones – "may they be happy!" Easy going so far, so one extends it to neutrals, people one knows but has no feelings about either way – "may they be happy!" (Vism IX.8–13). Now for enemies, that is to say, people who have done wicked things or been hostile. Here is where the work gets strenuous, and Buddhaghosa offers numerous strategies with the expectation that not all of them will necessarily succeed for any particular practitioner.

One technique is to admonish oneself that resentment only gratifies one's enemy because it makes one ugly, "prey to anger," and prone to harmful, mean actions (the techniques found in this and the following paragraph are from Vism IX.15–24). If that does not work, then one should try to find something decent and redeemable in the enemy that can be admired, and such admiration can be the seed of warmer feelings toward him. But if nothing worthy about the enemy can be found, then one should feel compassion for them, because someone with nothing at all decent about them is pitiable and destined for a hard time in this life and the next. And compassion itself can dissolve antipathy. Should this fail to do the trick, one should engage in various forms of self-admonishment, remonstrating with oneself that one's real enemy is not the other person, but anger itself, and that intransigent anger is corrosive to all of one's virtues and hopes. Why then continue to protect and nourish it? "This anger that you entertain is gnawing at the very roots of all the virtues that you guard – who is such a fool as you?" (Vism IX.22). One should realize how painful and punishing anger is to oneself. Further, given the transient and ever-changing nature of persons, the person one became angry with has now changed, and yet one continues to grasp and fix a rigid notion of them based on their original offense. So, one should reflect on the changeability of persons. If this fails, one should turn next to reflections on karma, remembering that one "is heir to one's actions" and that toxic intentions and actions of ill will can only mire one in bad future states in samsara.

More techniques may be needed if the anger and hatred stubbornly persist. One can deploy the "recollections of the Buddha" at this point to foster admiration and awe at the hard-won moral perfection of the Buddha, which Buddhaghosa relates by telling some of the great stories about him as he cultivated the perfections in past lives. Here the pleasurable and wondrous vision of a radically altruistic ideal can supplant the petty grievances that otherwise constrict the heart. But suppose this does not work either, and it may not because one has become so habituated to the "slavery of this defilement." Then, Buddhaghosa recommends, one should do an exercise of imagination whereby one considers the beginningless nature of samsara and how all of us have been sojourning through it in various relationships with one another in the past. If this is the case, then one's enemy now may have been one's mother or father in a past life. And if this is admitted as possible, one should have these thoughts:

This person, it seems, as my mother in the past carried me in her womb for ten months and removed from me without disgust, as if it were yellow sandalwood, my urine, excrement, spittle, snot, etc., and played with me on her lap, and nourished me, carrying me about on her hip (Vism IX.36).

Here one imagines oneself as a vulnerable infant and the enemy as one's nurturing mother who cared for one in these most visceral ways, an imaginative practice that radically reconsiders the other and the relationship. Buddhaghosa goes on to suggest that one can alternatively imagine the enemy as one's loving father in a distant lifetime, who traveled and toiled to support his children; or one may imagine the enemy as a former sister, brother, or other caregiver, allowing any of these relationships to become the basis for reconsidering the other in an entirely new way (and so the meditation does not rely on an idealized mother). Buddhaghosa then says merely that in the face of such poignant care carried out in that distant life, to continue to hate this person now would be "unbecoming."

We may notice further psychological depth in this exercise, in that even as one comes to see the other in a new light, one's own subjectivity is radically reconfigured. In the exercise one must contemplate one's own vulnerability as an infant incapable of removing even one's own excrement and completely reliant upon the care of others (indeed, human infants are totally helpless for quite a long time). Recognizing one's vulnerability and incapacity while yet being so gently nurtured may promote both gratitude and a tenderness toward that vulnerability and the image of being loved. These are important conditions for loving others.

Yet it may be that even this imaginative practice will fail, and so one should review the benefits of lovingkindness, which include, among many things, sleeping well, pleasant dreams, being loved by others, being able to concentrate, and dying peacefully (Vism IX.37–39). If this fails, one can do a meditation that is used for other purposes to dismantle a person into constituent parts to realize that the enemy is nothing more than an assemblage of constantly changing processes. So what is there to be angry with? This practice of "no-self" – seeing the manifold ways that persons are not ultimate, enduring selves or essences – is a fundamental insight in all forms of Buddhism, and here we see it deployed to dismantle anger, an emotion that attaches to a fixed, holistic, and often caricatured conception of the other. If none of these practices work, then as a last resort, Buddhaghosa recommends giving a gift – an act of spontaneous generosity can often succeed in interrupting one's petty ill will and bad feeling. When one has succeeded in dismantling resentment and begun feeling lovingkindness toward this enemy, one can then start with another person and so gradually extend the scope of the feeling.

Cultivating compassion involves finding a person in abject misery for whom compassion will easily flow and then longing that their suffering end. This can include those who are criminals and wrongdoers because their suffering will be horrendous if not in this life then in the next as karmic justice goes, inexorably, into effect (Vism IX.78–79). Compassion is not limited to innocents suffering unjustly, and the question of innocence or guilt does not even get raised here (though we should note that from a karmic perspective, no one is truly innocent and the apparent misfortunate that befalls them now may be the consequence of bad action in a previous life). This stance contrasts to many (but not all) Western philosophers starting with Aristotle, who reserve compassion for those subject to "undeserved" misfortune (as described by Nussbaum 2001, 301).

Sympathetic joy works at uprooting envy to take the happiness we readily share with our friends and expanding it to share in the happiness of all (and may be helpfully compared with Adam Smith's treatment of sympathy, as in Heim 2006). Equanimity is a practice of impartiality primarily to achieve peace. Potentially, it might also be enlisted to foster the experience of equality should one wish to develop constructively these exercises into an ethic of social justice (in ways that Buddhaghosa, notably, does not do).

As we wrap up this treatment of the sublime abidings and the exercises in Buddhaghosa's Concentration section, several general points are worth reiterating. The exercises, though not advanced on the basis of moral principle or even configured as part of morality as such, comprise the therapeutic development that constitutes the teleological transformation of the meditator. They develop perception and attention to help one to see further and with more clarity and concern because they help one look beyond the usual desires and aversions that distort one's vision and oppose one's freedom. In that sense the love yielded by these practices of attention is liberating.

2.3 Understanding

While starting to edge out of our range of concerns, Buddhaghosa's section on Understanding warrants some attention to sketch out fully the framework in which his moral thinking takes place. Understanding (*paññā*), the action of wise knowing seen as liberating, is the practice *and* the culmination of the path. Buddhaghosa defines understanding as something of "many sorts and with various aspects," but that includes "knowing in a particular mode separate from the modes of perceiving and cognizing" (Vism XIV.2–3). It is one thing to observe a red flower or the face of a loved one. However, understanding means that one does not just see the red flower, but knows that one *is* seeing the red flower and knows *how* one sees it: One notices that one is perceiving, and notices precisely the perceptual, affective, cognitive, and other types of phenomena that go into one's perception of the flower. In other words, one is able to identify, in a "meta" way, the processes of awareness, that is, all the phenomena that make up experience, and one knows their fleeting nature.

This is not known abstractly as one would be taking it in asserting that such and such abstract categories of phenomena exist; rather, the presence and workings of such phenomena are observed existentially or phenomenologically as one comes to understand one's moments of experience in context. This capacity to become aware of the phenomena of psychological life means that one notices the presence of, for example, feeling, as and how it occurs when one gazes, say, at the face of a loved one. This definition of understanding does not entail the imputing of any sort of ontological essence to these phenomena, as is sometimes assumed in the scholarship. Rather, it is to be aware of the features that make up one's awareness, and in this sense, understanding is a kind of meta-awareness that is itself said to be liberating.

It is in light of these considerations that we may note briefly Buddhaghosa's reading of the scriptural corpus of material known as the Abhidhamma, because he took it to provide the very disciplinary practices that constitute this kind of understanding. The Abhidhamma consists of a range of different styles of inquiry, but most prominently it offers extensive matrices of the phenomena said to be present in moments of conscious experience. The phenomena analyzed include the sorts of psychological processes we have been considering: feeling, perceptual judgment, intention, and so on (up to long open-ended lists of more than fifty different phenomena). These phenomena are treated in the Abhidhamma through highly modal and modular practices of analysis that consider, and reconsider, how they occur in relation to other phenomena in the complex and constantly shifting vicissitudes of moment-by-moment experience. For example, "feeling" (*vedanā*) is present in all moments of awareness, but varies depending on what other phenomena occur along with it in any given moment, whereby feeling may be pleasurable, painful, or neutral, and indeed further divided into more finely grained varieties where useful and relevant (Vism XIV.125–128).

In addition to offering many matrices of the various phenomena that can be present in distinct moments of awareness, the Abhidhamma also offers specific methods of analysis through which they can be analyzed further, specifically, doctrines like the Eightfold Path, the Four Truths, the five "aggregates" that comprise a person, dependent origination, the four practices of mindfulness, the four sublime abidings, and so on.[9] All of these analyze phenomena to show their workings and interrelatedness, and to provide therapeutic understanding and

---

[9] Among the seven books of the Abhidhamma, the *Dhammasaṅgaṇī* gives the long matrices of phenomena; the *Vibhaṅga* gives eighteen specific methods of analysis of which several are mentioned here.

methods to change them. We have already discussed some of these, and others will take us further afield than we have room to go. But by way of an example, we can consider the five aggregates that are said to comprise a person.

The "five aggregates" is a doctrine that analyzes the phenomenality of a person into five clusters or "aggregates" of constantly changing phenomena: form, perceptual judgment, feeling, mental constructions, and awareness (and all of these can be analyzed further) (Vism ch. XIV). "Form" includes all of the phenomena of our subjective experience of materiality; "perceptual judgment" is the ways we perceive and label parts of our experience; "feeling" is the hedonic or affective responses we give to it; "mental constructions" are a huge category of psychological tendencies, habits, and dispositions that shape intentionality; and "awareness" is moment-by-moment constantly changing consciousness. By breaking up our usually more fixed and stable notions of "person" into these five constantly changing collections of phenomena, this doctrinal method is considered salutary for those who construct and reify a notion of unchanging personhood, an eternal or essential self or soul, or a rigid notion of one's own or others' identities (which Buddhists think is most of us most of the time). By breaking down the person into its aggregate parts, and by breaking down those aggregates further, one can replace deeply entrenched notions of selfhood with more finely grained sets of processes that allow the practitioner to acquire knowledge into their causal workings. Knowing the causal workings of such processes allows one to make changes in one's experience at a very fine level. This is the very sort of understanding that Buddhaghosa sees as liberating. It should also be noted that the five aggregates is just one mode, among others, used to break down the person to look more closely at causal conditions underlying it. Another key mode is dependent origination, which breaks down the person differently into twelve clusters of causal phenomena.[10] In proper modal fashion, there is no single way to practice this kind of anatomizing of the human person.

For Buddhaghosa then, the Abhidhamma is an inexhaustible and oceanic series of such "methods" (*naya*) that can be deployed for analyzing the content of experience (Pe Maung Tin 1999: 20). This conception of the Abhidhamma differs substantially from the Indian Abhidharma systems, those geographically located most likely in Gandhara, which had a decidedly more ontological thrust (see Bronkhorst 2018; on the Pali Abhidhamma tradition see Heim, forthcoming), and scholars should avoid conflating the two traditions. The Pali tradition was not engaged in a reductive ontology of these phenomena that would lead to a notion

---

[10] Dependent origination involves an analysis of the causal interrelations of the phenomena of human experience that maps out twelve links of phenomena, especially in how they work over time: ignorance, mental constructions, awareness, name-and-form, the six senses, contact, feeling, craving, clinging, becoming, birth, and aging-and-death (Vism ch. XVII).

that feeling and the other categories of phenomena could be seen in essentialist or reified terms as the ultimate units of reality. Rather, the practices of understanding that Buddhaghosa describes in his last section of the *Path of Purification* consist of analytical modes of dismantling phenomena and reclassifying them according to the classifications and relationships of causality that define them.

Because the early Pali Abhidhamma does not endeavor to assert or establish the phenomena of experience as ultimate reals, it cannot be the target of the Madhyamaka critique launched against the north Indian Abhidharma traditions initiated by Nāgārjuna and carried forward by Śāntideva. The Madhyamaka tradition, which we will consider extensively in Śāntideva's formulation shortly, critiqued the north Indian Abhidharma ontologies for essentializing and reifying the phenomena (*dharmas*) arrived at through its various practices of reduction. The Madhyamaka thinkers attempted to show that these phenomena, indeed all things, are "empty" of unchanging, fixed, and unconditioned essences, only coming into being and properly understood within a network of causes and conditions. "Emptiness" thus becomes a central teaching for this school.

Although Buddhaghosa is by no means a Madhyamaka and his intellectual practices are altogether different from Madhyamaka styles of critique and argument (and different also from those of its targets), he did use ideas of the emptiness of *dhammas* as a matter of course, and the canonical Abhidhamma texts also were aware of emptiness as a mode of analysis. For Buddhaghosa emptiness practice is a contemplation that sees the phenomena (*dhammas*) of experiential life as "empty," that is "lacking essence."[11] For him, phenomena can be usefully seen as "empty" of essence or any sort of permanent and fixed being, including the aspectual definitions of morality that we have considered.[12] The phenomena of the five aggregates are also "empty" (Vism XX.20, XXI.60), as are the phenomena described by the Four Noble Truths (Vism XVI.14), for example. Although not showcased as a singularly powerful technique or principle as it is by Śāntideva (as we will see), emptiness for Buddhaghosa is one contemplative practice, among many others, for analyzing all kinds of phenomena and one "doorway," among others, to liberation.[13]

---

[11] "'These are just *dhammas*' is said to show that, due to their emptiness, 'they are only *dhammas*, without essence, without a leader'" (*dhammāva ete dhammamattā asārā apariṇāyakāti imissā suññatāya dīpanatthaṃ vuttā, Atthasālinī* 155). I translate and quote the Pali here for Buddhism specialists for whom Buddhaghosa's views on emptiness are not well known.

[12] Vism I.140 deploys a long list of contemplations to analyze and define one aspectual classification of *sīla*, that is morality as abandoning, refraining, intention, restraint, and nontransgression (I.19); one of these many contemplations is studying these "through the contemplation of emptiness " (*suññatānupassanāya*).

[13] Vism XXI.67–71; he is getting this from the *Paṭisambhidāmagga* (Ps ii.48). There is said to be three "doorways to freedom" (*vimokkhamukha*) – three ways of achieving liberation: freedom

This is all to suggest that a key Buddhist insight – that all things are to be seen as contingent and conditioned and thus as devoid of independent, self-existent, essential nature – has many pathways to realization. In many ways the deconstructive work of emptiness can be seen as a corollary of Buddhaghosa's modal or aspectual analyses, which are at work throughout the *Path of Purification*. Every item of teaching or phenomenon of experience can be picked up and analyzed in various modes, flipped over, and reconsidered from other aspects, and defined variously through matrices that lead to other matrices. When I identify the greed or the anger that is shaping my awareness, for example, I can stand outside of it, see its conditions and ultimate insubstantiality, and thus be liberated from it. This is what it is to develop understanding as well as contemplative techniques. It also is a practice that resists attributing any single essence to any phenomenon, for if there are always multiple modes of analyzing and defining something, there is no single, final, viewed-from-nowhere essence of it. For Buddhaghosa, as an Analyst, this work of modal analysis purifies both the moral life and the most important and liberating kinds of human understanding.

3 Śāntideva and an Ethic of Radical Compassion

Śāntideva lived nearly three centuries after Buddhaghosa and in a very different philosophical context. As in the case of Buddhaghosa, much of what we know about his life is shrouded in legend. But it is clear that Śāntideva was a major exponent of the Madhyamaka school, which was one philosophical tradition within the larger movement of the Mahayana that had by his day become well established in north India. He studied and composed his work at Nālandā University, perhaps the largest university in the world at the time, and his work has proved highly influential in Tibetan Buddhism.

Several features of the Mahayana movement must be noted at the outset to make sense of Śāntideva's project. The Mahayana was not a *school* of Buddhism, but rather a series of interventions and innovations that shifted points of emphasis, orientation, and aspiration; these interventions can be traced historically to apocryphal scriptures (sutras), such as the Perfection of Wisdom sutras that emerged around the first century of the Common Era, and eventually developed into a copious literature of Mahayana texts that in some cases came to have devotional followings. (We should note that the linguistic world at this point is Sanskrit, as we shift away from the scriptural and commentarial corpus in Pali, the language of the Theravada, which was little used in India at this time.)

---

by the signless (*animittavimokkha*); freedom by desirelessness (*appaṇihita*); and freedom by emptiness (*suññatā*).

The new scriptures did not entirely supplant the earlier canons among the adherents of Mahayana ideas, but they were given higher status, and the earlier bodies of material (and those who would limit textual authority to them) were sometimes cast in highly polemical terms. In addition, the work of the second century CE philosopher Nāgārjuna on emptiness in this early period was also crucial for the philosophical development of the Mahayana in the forms it took thereafter, including the transmissions of Buddhism to China and the rest of East Asia, and, later, to Tibet.

The two most important innovations of the Mahayana involved the development of the bodhisattva ideal, especially its emphasis on universal compassion, and the foregrounding of philosophical ideas about emptiness. Both are central to Śāntideva's thought. We can consider the bodhisattva ideal first. In "mainstream" Buddhism (what modern scholars call the non-Mahayana systems of Indian Buddhism, which can include the Theravada), the Buddha was held to be a moral exemplar and teacher of the path to liberation. His long journey to buddhahood that took innumerable previous lives to achieve is instructive, awe-inspiring, and highly valued, but was not generally considered something ordinary people could emulate (instead, practitioners seek to become *arhats*, liberated persons who are not at the level of buddhas). During his previous lives practicing the perfections prerequisite for his discovering and teaching the Buddhist truths and path, he was called a "bodhisattva" (Pali, *bodhisatta*), that is, a buddha-in-training. In a departure from these views, the early Mahayana scriptures begin to suggest that the Buddha's life, including his long path as a bodhisattva, could be followed more widely, and they came to promote this path for all practitioners.

What makes the bodhisattva path notable is that it was not concerned solely with liberation, or release from the suffering of rebirth, karma, and removing the toxic defilements, as is the *arhat* path of purification and soteriological freedom articulated by Buddhaghosa. All agree that what the Buddha achieved was not only this, but also the capacity to discover the truths in the first place, to teach them, and thus to save others.[14] The goal of a bodhisattva is to achieve the perfections that fostered the discovery of the truths and the practices that can release people from suffering in samsara (for Śāntideva there are six perfections to the Theravada's ten: generosity, morality, forbearance, vigor, meditation, and understanding). When becoming a buddha is the goal (rather than becoming "just" an *arhat* free of samsara), then the perfections, and above all the compassion that fundamentally characterizes this higher goal, become the path. Further,

---

[14] Actually, it was not really "in the first place": Buddhist teachings claim that there were innumerable buddhas before our Buddha who discovered and taught the truths, but that their dispensations had been forgotten and our Buddha rediscovered and taught them. His dispensation will also someday be lost and will be rediscovered by a future buddha.

the path becomes much longer: Although becoming an *arhat* is at least conceivable in one lifetime, the path of the bodhisattva, modeled on the Buddha's countless past lives of striving for ethical and spiritual perfection, becomes considerably protracted. As a Mahayana thinker, Śāntideva aims not at the path of purification to achieve individual liberation of an *arhat* (as in the case of Buddhaghosa), but at this much grander and exalted ideal of saving all beings. Thus, as we consider Śāntideva's ethical thought, we will be concerned with questions of altruism and universal compassion, and challenging issues of self-sacrifice and radically altruistic ethical ideals that are constitutive of this higher vision.

The second major innovation of the Mahayana is the development of emptiness teachings, as we have already begun to describe. As we have seen, emptiness was not unknown to the Theravada. Buddhaghosa uses emptiness as a practice to break down not only persons but also the phenomena that constitute them; it is a mode of contemplative and analytical practice, among others, for understanding and liberation. But in the Perfection of Wisdom Sutras and in Nāgārjuna's philosophical work, emptiness becomes a fundamental philosophical stance, and Nāgārjuna initially (and Śāntideva six centuries later) deploys epistemological argumentation to establish an understanding of all phenomena as conditioned and conditioning and thus "empty" of inherent, self-contained, independent essences. Madhyamaka philosophers argued against north Indian Abhidharma traditions that they interpreted as positing an ontology of ultimate reality, and Śāntideva is building on a long history of formal metaphysical and epistemological reasoning to dismantle such metaphysical views. Traditional and modern scholars alike argue about whether the outcome of this philosophical work results in a position about ultimate reality – that all things are empty – or whether it, at the end of the day, dismantles all such positions including emptiness itself.

By the time of the mature Madhyamaka of the eighth century – Śāntideva's moment – philosophical debate about metaphysical questions had become highly advanced. Also robust was philosophical development in logic and epistemology as Buddhists of various stripes at Nālandā university debated with one another and non-Buddhist interlocutors; advances in what we would call Hindu philosophical systems were equally rigorous, and the debates between many different systems were critical to the sophistication of the entire classical Indian philosophical tradition. This situation contrasts quite sharply with Buddhaghosa, who was either innocent of these philosophical developments in India in his day or saw his project as an Analyst as fundamentally different in nature and in scope.

These considerations entail important metaethical implications as we try to understand the forms that ethical thought took in ancient Buddhism. I have argued that Buddhaghosa does not attempt to ground his ethical project via metaphysical argumentation, and instead offers a pragmatic investigation and transformation of experience based on a disciplinary study of phenomenology. To be sure, as a Buddhist, he is doctrinally committed to Buddhism (as is Śāntideva, of course), but when we consider the nature of his intellectual work, we do not find him engaged in metaphysical or epistemological argumentation that attempts to establish an ontology, the nature of reality, what ultimately exists or does not exist, or how we know this. He does not argue for a metaphysical position as a foundation for his phenomenology (though he may assume one), nor does he use his phenomenological practice to establish a metaphysics. We often find him working with no-self and emptiness, but when we draw back and consider the ways in which these are being deployed, we find them always operating as disciplinary practices of analyzing experience, rather than as positions about reality or what exists as matters to be established via philosophical argumentation. This may be considered an important weakness in his thought from a certain point of view. That is to say, once within his doctrinal commitments and the basic assumptions of his tradition, Buddhaghosa's system is ingenious. But as he offers no attempt to ground a view of reality, it may not convince others outside of its foundational assumptions of any claim for universal relevance.

Śāntideva, on the other hand, does appear to attempt to ground, or at least support, his ethical program in a series of metaphysical arguments about reality and is more ambitious in this sense. As a Madhyamaka, he endorses emptiness, and he sets about arguing for this position against a wide variety of opponents, most obviously in chapter 9 of *How to Lead an Awakened Life*. It is on the basis of these arguments for an emptiness position or perspective that he propounds his spiritual exercises. He states clearly: "there is no valid objection to the emptiness position (*śūnyatāpakṣa*). Therefore, emptiness should be meditated on without reservation" (BCA 9.53).[15] Though he is careful to assert that ultimate insight into reality involves spiritual liberation through a fundamental transformation in one's whole way of seeing, a realization that is in an important sense ineffable and beyond intellection, he still practices rational argumentation to facilitate understanding of that reality.

A key distinction in the Mahayana context relevant here is the distinction between "ultimate" and "conventional" truth. For Śāntideva, this distinction concerns what can be asserted coherently and consistently. We use conventional truth in everyday life as we mention people and things that upon further analysis

---

[15] All translations of the *Bodhicaryāvatāra* (BCA) are Crosby and Skilton's (2008), though I cite them by chapter and verse rather than page number. I follow Garfield's apt rendering of the title as *How to Lead an Awakened Life* (Garfield 2010).

dissolve into smaller and highly conditioned components. In this sense, though
necessary for ordinary conversation and true within its terms, conventional truth
is only provisional and so is, ultimately or from the standpoint of ultimate truth,
illusory. I may need to use the words "I" and "myself" to get through an
ordinary day, but from the standpoint of emptiness, and thus ultimate truth,
these are reified constructions and conventions that have no substantial, inherent, or independent truth. Indeed, the force of emptiness teachings is that they
ruthlessly dismantle *all* concepts and phenomena in such terms to indicate that
they are all conventional, and thus in some sense false or delusional (the word
used for conventional, *saṃvṛti,* means concealing). Ultimate truth, then, lies
behind such conceptual reifications and it involves dismantling them. As
Śāntideva puts it, "truth (*tattvam*) is beyond the scope of intellection.
Intellection is said to be the conventional" (BCA 9.2).

Yet even while he enjoins the practitioner to meditate on emptiness (because
ultimately emptiness is a way of seeing that eludes conceptualization),
Śāntideva also attempts to foster understanding of it by way of the philosophical
arguments that constitute chapter 9. Of course, the notion of emptiness is itself
mired in intellection and thus does not escape the analysis – in this sense, all
views, even emptiness, are empty of intrinsic truth (and the Madhyamaka
thinkers encouraged this paradoxical realization). Still, he mounts arguments
that can help the practitioner understand emptiness and that aim at disputing
those who held other views. Throughout he uses formulations about truth
(*tattva, satya*) and arguments about what does and does not exist (*asti* and *na
asti*) (e.g. BCA 9.107, 111). He advances epistemological arguments in defense
of the Madhyamaka position on emptiness. Further, he is exclusivist about the
emptiness position: "scripture states there is no awakening without this path"
(BCA 9.40). Unlike in Buddhaghosa's work where emptiness is one mode of
contemplative analysis that can be liberating (among others), emptiness is *the*
key insight into truth and awakening for Śāntideva.

The contrast with Buddhaghosa on the use of the conventional/ultimate
distinction is instructive. Buddhaghosa sometimes deploys a distinction
between the Buddha's more common-parlance (*vohara*) or customary (*sammuti*) language or teachings on the one hand, and his "furthest-sense" (*para-
mattha*) language or teachings that involve reductive analysis on the other.[16]
The Buddha sometimes spoke about practices like lovingkindness and

---

[16] The Pali word for conventional language is *sammuti,* which is not cognate with Sanskrit *saṃvṛti*
and bears no sense of concealing reality. When Buddhaghosa speaks of the distinction, it is not
about truth, reality, or what exists but about the Buddha's language (*bhāsa*) or teachings (*kathā*)
and their purposes and contexts (*Manorathapūraṇī* I.94–96; *Papañcasūdanī* I.137–138; See
Heim 2018, 85–94, for translation and discussion of these passages).

compassion that depend on some conventional notion of persons, but he could also speak more technically and analytically to dismantle such ideas if the situation required it for effective teaching. But importantly, for Buddhaghosa these distinctions about language are not about *truth* or *what exists*; they instead concern different registers of the Buddha's teachings. Because they characterize the Buddha's teachings they are equally true, since everything the Buddha taught is of course (for Buddhaghosa) fully and completely true. In other words, the distinction does not concern truth or ontology in early Theravada as it does in Mahayana thought.

All of this is to note a contrast between Buddhaghosa and Śāntideva to the effect that the latter is engaged in epistemological argumentation to establish metaphysical support for his ethical thought. As Jay Garfield puts it, for Śāntideva "metaphysics and epistemology are central to our moral lives" and compassion is "the direct result of a genuine appreciation of the essencelessness and interdependence of all sentient beings" (Garfield 2016: 89–90). This style of ethics whereby ethical positions and practices are explicitly grounded in (or at least supported by) metaphysical argumentation is much more familiar to many Western ethicists than the type of work Buddhaghosa is doing. This may be one possible reason why Śāntideva has attracted more attention from Western scholars working on ethics than any other Indian Buddhist thinker except (perhaps) for the Buddha himself.[17] Buddhaghosa's program of phenomenological analysis has proved more elusive to grasp, and some thinkers, when they have considered the issue at all, have been skeptical that one can even proceed with an ethical program without a metaphysics (e.g. Lele 2015). (But to be sure, not all Western ethics is based on metaphysics.) Buddhaghosa, as I have tried to suggest, offers a way to think about how to live starting and ending with studying phenomenology. Of course, his phenomenology is hardly without presuppositions and normative value, as it is framed by the Buddhist teleological project; but it is not undergirded by metaphysical or epistemological argument.

That said, in many instances Śāntideva deploys methods very similar to Buddhaghosa's, and the differences in philosophical style should not obscure some of the patterns of shared practice we see across the Indic Buddhist tradition mentioned in the introduction section. Like Buddhaghosa, Śāntideva

---

[17] There is substantial scholarly work on Śāntideva; to list just some of it: Clayton 2006, 2009; Gyatso 2005, 2009; Edelglass 2017; Flores 2008, ch. 9; Garfield 2010; Goodman 2009, 2016; Harris 2017; Todd 2013; Lele 2015; Mrozik 2007; Williams 1998. It should be noted that some scholars of Madhyamaka have been skeptical that the Madhyamaka is attempting to establish a metaphysical view of ultimate reality at all (e.g. Siderits 2016; Westerhoff 2016), or that if it is doing so, that ethical views can logically follow from it (e.g. Williams 1998; Jenkins 2016).

is articulating (and indeed inhabiting as we will see with BCA) a spiritual path that is largely a matter of moral phenomenology, examining one's subjectivity and changing one's entire psychology. As with Buddhaghosa, the journey is fundamentally a matter of examining one's subjectivity and transforming one's ways of perceiving, feeling, and attending. But with Śāntideva we also have to take into consideration the metaphysical arguments he gives in relationship to the phenomenology and the practices that he explores. And because he gives such arguments, we are invited to engage them.

Further, a word or two should be said concerning the relationship of Śāntideva and Buddhaghosa because much of the Mahayana tradition that Śāntideva was part of was highly polemical in its treatment of what they called the "Way of the Disciples" or the "Lesser Vehicle" traditions with which the Theravada by default gets lumped (in that the Theravada did not accept the Mahayana scriptures or claims). Because Buddhaghosa lived three centuries before Śāntideva and because Śāntideva's school was quite critical of non-Mahayana traditions, it might seem that Śāntideva is critiquing Buddhaghosa's path either explicitly or implicitly. But historically the matter is more complicated than this, not least because it is by no means evident that the Mahayana scriptures knew of or critiqued the Theravada in any of its formulations. The development of the Theravada took place in Sri Lanka and at some remove from the world of Śāntideva, his precursors, and the philosophical debates and development occurring in his period in India. Śāntideva was an extremely learned man who authored an anthology of Buddhist texts drawing from at least seventy-eight different sources, none of which were the *Visuddhimagga*, Buddhaghosa's commentaries, or any of the Pali scriptures. Nor is it easy to recognize in any of Śāntideva's opponents, as he lays them out in chapter 9, a position that corresponds to Buddhaghosa's work. So it would be unwarranted to see Śāntideva as arguing against Buddhaghosa in any obvious or direct way.

For his part, Buddhaghosa was originally from India and was surely aware of the growing prominence of the Mahayana in his own day and the fecundity of the philosophical traditions taking place in monastic centers of learning like Nālandā. Though he seems to have been acquainted with some of the ideas associated with the Mahayana, he avoids (we may assume purposefully) directly engaging the debates of his contemporaries in India. These considerations suggest that we regard Buddhaghosa and Śāntideva, and the two traditions they represent (Theravada orthodoxy in the first case, and a mature formulation of Madhyamaka philosophy in the second), as nonintersecting lines of development. They clearly draw from some of the same wells of Buddhist thought and practice, but they are not speaking directly to each other.

3.1 How to Lead an Awakened Life

Śāntideva wrote two texts that have survived: *How to Lead an Awakened Life* (BCA) and *Training Anthology* (ŚS).[18] These are quite different works. *How to Lead an Awakened Life* is a lyrically beautiful account of the spiritual journey of taking and realizing the bodhisattva vow – the aspiration to work tirelessly to achieve the perfections and cultivate universal compassion. It is a sequenced meditation on how to generate the motivation for compassion for all beings to the point, at least for those who reach the highest echelons of achievement, of total self-sacrifice. The protagonist is Śāntideva himself writing in a confessional register as he battles his demons and exhorts himself to rise to this most extraordinary ambition. The text eludes easy classification as it advances through stylized liturgical worship and confession, spiritual exercises (many of which are quite similar to Buddhaghosa's), pages and pages of emotionally wrought self-admonishment, and then highly technical philosophical argument. It is among the most poignantly personal and psychologically probing texts in all of Buddhist literature and one of its finest literary pieces. In contrast, *Training Anthology* is an anthology of other texts, carefully crafted and structured as Śāntideva draws from a huge range of Mahayana sources to fashion an interpretation of the structure of the Buddhist life, and as a compendium it is largely not his own writing. We will focus on *How to Lead an Awakened Life* as a structured ethical path, but from time to time will supplement its treatment of key issues with *Training Anthology*.

The bodhisattva vow is lovingly expressed by Śāntideva in this plea that comes at the end of *How to Lead an Awakened Life*:

> As long as space abides and as long as the world abides, so long may I abide, destroying the sufferings of the world (BCA 10.55).

The aspiring bodhisattva yearns to linger in samsara even for countless eons in order to practice compassion for all beings and ultimately perfect his or her character. Readers should not imagine that this is hyperbole: Śāntideva's heart-felt plea is in earnest and he has toiled for 900 verses of two lines each, restructuring his entire outlook and moral sensibility so that this aspiration alone remains as the most obvious, indeed the only, option available. How does he arrive at this?

To see how he gets here, we will follow, in summary fashion, the stages of this transformation. As in Buddhaghosa's path, this journey involves the deepest psychological probing to ferret out impurities, defilements, and obscurations. But in Śāntideva's case it is presented in the first person as *his* spiritual journey. The

---

[18] Goodman 2016 offers a welcome new translation of *Training Anthology* (*Śikṣā-samuccaya*) and all references to it are his translations, cited as ŚS with Goodman's page numbers.

path involves concrete, albeit highly stylized, exercises of imagination, self-remonstration, and cognitive therapy to shift his perspective, cultivate attention, dismantle harmful feelings, facilitate beneficial feelings, and achieve new ways of knowing and seeing. Along the way we will delve into some of the philosophical intricacies of emptiness teachings to see if and how they undergird this path. We will also linger over some of the challenges posed by this ethic of self-sacrificial altruism and generosity, and the very exalted standards set by this most extraordinary ideal.

How to Lead an Awakened Life begins with a Mahayana liturgy of worship and confession. Śāntideva starts by praising the buddhas and bodhisattvas that have come before him. He recognizes that this moment holds an opportunity to grasp and seize the "awakening mind" (*bodhicitta*), that is, the motivation to practice universal compassion for all time, a new way of seeing that involves a fundamental shift in attention and awareness. This mind or awareness is of two kinds: aspirational (the work of generating the motivation) and engaged (the work of protecting, purifying, and maintaining it once committed) (BCA 1.16). It is no small matter to generate the will to save all beings at whatever cost as the chief aim and ambition of one's life (and future lives), and then one must live committed to it, ever unflagging in one's efforts. Śāntideva is all too aware of what an extraordinary vow he is taking. It even becomes something of a mystery to him that he is even able to think of such a thing and to realistically aspire to it: He is like a blind man who has "somehow" found a jewel in a rubbish heap (BCA 3.27). In places he suggests that it is only through the mysterious workings of the Buddha that he is able to even conceive it: The awakening mind occurs "like a flash of lightning in the dark of night" cutting through the obscurations of his awareness by the power of the Buddha (BCA 1.5).

So he worships and praises the lineage of buddhas and bodhisattvas whose ranks he hopes to join. In the face of their flawless virtues, he comes to feel his own unworthiness and depravity, whereupon he shifts into a confessional register of utmost contrition, self-effacement, and anguish. Here we must quote his verses to convey something of the literary and confessional quality of his writing.

> Throughout the beginingless cycle of existence, and again in this very birth,
>   the evil I, a brute, have done or caused,
> Or anything I, deluded, have rejoiced in to my own detriment, I confess that
>   transgression, tormented by remorse.
> The cruel evil I have wickedly done, corrupted by many faults; O leaders,
>   I confess it all (BCA 2.28, 29, 31).

As he confesses he becomes even more acutely aware of the evils he has done and of which he is yet capable. He ponders the inevitable encroachment of death and his vulnerability to the effects of his own actions in the relentless causality of karma until he finds himself cowering with a "feverish horror, which grips me covered in my own uncontrolled excrement, as Death's terrifying messengers stand over me" (BCA 2.45). In the depths of his fear and torment he seeks refuge in the great buddhas and bodhisattvas whose infinite compassion can support and sustain him in a new, radically altered, mode of life.

By chapter 3 he has settled into relief from his confession, gratitude for the compassion of the saviors, and a fresh resolve to make a new day of it. He rejoices at the happiness and beneficence of the awakened mind as he begins the bodhisattva vow:

> With the good acquired by doing all this as described, may I allay the suffering of every living being.
> I am medicine for the sick. May I be both doctor and their nurse, until the sickness does not recur.
> May I avert the pain of hunger and thirst with showers of food and drink. May I become both drink and food in the intermediate aeons of famine.
> I make over my body to all embodied beings to do with as they please. Let them continually beat it, insult it, and splatter it with filth.
> Let them play with my body; let them be derisive and amuse themselves. I have given this body to them. What point has this concern of mine? (BCA 3.6, 7, 12, 13).

His taking of the vow in these verses (and others that continue in the same vein) indicates that he is prepared to give every help to beings in whatever manner their miseries might be allayed. His body can nourish the hungry and his merit can serve all needs. He offers some reasoning for this: "abandonment of all is Enlightenment and Enlightenment is my heart's goal. If I must give up everything, better to be given to sentient beings" (BCA 3.11). Here generosity and renunciation come together – if I am to strip away all attachment to achieve the freedom of nirvana, I might as well use whatever I may have to benefit others. He ends the chapter on a note of great rejoicing for having joined the lineage of buddhas.

Śāntideva now sobers up as he contemplates the enormity of his vow, the vast gap between his aspirations and his present moral condition, and the horrors that will follow a broken vow should he fail to live up to it. His vow has made him more acutely aware than ever of his shortcomings, and he grimly takes the measure of his defilements, his "enemies" that lead to hell.

> Though I have somehow come to a nigh unattainable place of advantage, and though I understand this, still I am led back to those selfsame hells once more.
>
> I have no will in this matter, as if bewildered by spells. I do not understand. By what am I perplexed? Who dwells here within me?
>
> Enemies such as greed and hate lack hands and feet and other limbs. They are not brave, nor are they wise. How is it they enslave me? (BCA 4.26–28).

In despair he looks within to find enemies – greed and hatred – that enslave him (the notion of being enslaved by one's defilements is of course familiar from Buddhaghosa). This aspiring bodhisattva looks within to find demons of confusion and toxic desires and aversions shackling his progress, and he swings wildly between the most exalted of aspirations and the depths of despair at his incapacity.

> I have promised to liberate the universe from the defilements, to the limit of space in the ten directions, but even my own self is not freed from the defilements!
>
> At that time I was intoxicated, speaking without realizing my own limitations. After that I can never turn back from destroying the defilements.
>
> I shall be tenacious in this, and wage war sworn to enmity, except against the kind of defilement that comes from murdering the defilements (BCA 4.41–43).

What to do but to gird his loins and join battle against the defilements?

And so he does: The remaining chapters engage the six perfections that wage war on their opposites. In a logic reminiscent of Buddhaghosa, attaining virtue is a matter of driving out vice: *Generosity* is getting rid of attachment; *morality* is avoiding harm to others; *forbearance* is being rid of anger and hatred; *vigor* is securing oneself against "sloth, clinging to what is vile, despondency, and self-contempt" (BCA 7.2); *meditation* is removing distraction; and *understanding* is removing false views. All of these are premised on "the guarding of awareness," and once again we are apprised that this moral path is, above all, a psychological reconstruction of one's attention and subjectivity. No evil can cease until the mind, which otherwise ruts and rampages like a mad elephant, is tamed and tethered by mindfulness (BCA 5.2–3).

At this point it may be fair to worry that the whole thing is a matter of intention and psychological transformation at the expense of actually doing things that change the world (and doing things that change the world would seem to be required by the promise to save all beings). Indeed, this text's actual treatment of the perfections of generosity and morality (*śīla*) is startlingly clipped and raises important concerns along these lines. On generosity he says only this:

> If the perfection of generosity consists of making the universe free from poverty, how can previous Protectors have acquired it, when the world is still poor, even today?
>
> The perfection of generosity is said to result from the mental attitude of relinquishing all that one has to all people, together with the fruit of that act. Therefore, the perfection is the mental attitude itself (BCA 5.9–10).

It is an intriguing conundrum that, despite countless bodhisattvas in past and present toiling for eons perfecting immeasurable generosity, poverty stubbornly persists in the world. But here is why: Generosity is a matter of motivation rather than achieving perfect conditions in the world. (It truly is "the thought that counts.") His treatment of morality (*śīla*), defined here as not harming, is similar:

> Where can fish and other creatures be taken where I might not kill them? Yet when the mental attitude to cease from worldly acts is achieved, that is agreed to be the perfection of morality (BCA 5.11).

This cry of anguish for the harm he wreaks, inevitably, on the creatures of the world indicates the difficulty of living in a truly harmless way toward the world. (It is an anguish to which we, in our time of unprecedented ecological devastation at human hands, can most certainly relate – *where indeed can the fish and other animals go to escape us?*) But morality is really a state of mind achieved while sitting on a meditation cushion, so that once the mental purification has been achieved, the perfection is achieved. The world may remain unruly but one can learn to control one's own mind: "since I cannot control external events, I will control my own mind. What concern is it of mine whether other things are controlled?" (BCA 5.14).

This ethic undoubtedly leaves Śāntideva vulnerable to critiques that would require moral transformation to issue in effective action in the world. Should the bodhisattva's *perfections* of generosity and morality lie solely in a trained mind? To be sure, a trained mind free of harmful intent will not issue in deliberate violence and destruction, and an unattached mind will surely yield an open hand. Later in this same chapter he advocates action: "one should always be able and energetic, at all times acting upon one's own initiative" and "in all actions one should not leave any work to another" (BCA 5.82; see also 7.63–66 for the sweetness and satisfaction a bodhisattva finds in action, and his thirst for moral tasks). In the last chapter of his text Śāntideva prays for the succoring of the poor and the end of all suffering in the world from the torments of animals being eaten to the pangs of women in labor. Perhaps in the early stages, generosity and morality are matters of mental control, but by the end of the journey he has considered the actions they entail for other beings. In *Training Anthology* Śāntideva elaborates the kinds of actual actions required by generosity and morality, and the notion of skillful means or effectiveness in the bodhisattva's doings receives much attention.

In the main body of the text, we find many strategies for getting the mind under control and weeding out the defilements. As with Buddhaghosa, many of these follow a logic of "antidotes": Forbearance is the antidote to anger; vigor is the antidote to sloth; disgust with the body is the antidote to lust. He also describes many of the same kinds of meditation techniques that we saw with Buddhaghosa, such as contemplating the disgustingness of the body, especially imagining it decayed, dismembered, and as food for vultures, to dislodge lust and attachment to the body (BCA 5.59–67; 8.30–33). In his chapter on the perfection of vigor – an essential perfection because the bodhisattva must never slacken his efforts from weariness, distraction, or laziness – Śāntideva, again like Buddhaghosa, evokes the hellfire that so often proves indispensable in religious and moral exhortation: Fear generates urgency. And in the chapter on meditative perfection, he labors to set aside the distractions of lust, pride, worldly pleasure, and self-love. In these verses, Śāntideva refines and perfects the art of self-admonishment, scolding himself for holding on to anger, lust, weakness, and folly despite his earnest entreaties to abandon them. In many ways the phenomenologies and methods of Buddhaghosa and Śāntideva are similar: Both explore with great nuance the painful afflictions of evil and fear, and the freer and happier ways of being when these are removed.

In these respects, Śāntideva's works are "meditation manuals," as William Edelglass describes them, leading to gradual, but quite radical, spiritual and moral transformation (Edelglass 2017, 227). As with the meditation work Buddhaghosa prescribes, Śāntideva develops subtle shifts of perception and affect, where one attends to others in a way that will diffuse one's anger and indifference toward them. Because anger and hatred are the most toxic and destructive emotions and even a flash of them destroys countless eons of hard bodhisattva work (BCA 6.1), Śāntideva offers numerous techniques to dismantle them so that if one fails another may succeed. For example, I (in that Śāntideva's first-person voice comes to include me) should note that anger is corrosive to my happiness, sleep, friendships, and peace of mind (BCA 6.3–6); the causes of my anger are themselves a matter of complex conditions with no ultimate agent or essence to target, so why not let it dissolve? (BCA 6.24–30); and my enemies have reasons and conditions driving them as they in their clumsy way seek to avoid suffering and achieve happiness – why not look with compassion instead of anger on their foolishness? (BCA 6.33–53). Why do I not instead consider the harm *I* have done them? (BCA 6.45–49). Moreover, our enemies teach us forbearance and so in this important sense they function as teachers helping us on the path – how then can we not worship them as equal in respect to the buddhas who have also taught the Teaching? (BCA 6.111–118). Further, a bodhisattva is not imperiled just by anger, but is also vulnerable to "pride, good repute, and honor" because he is on such an ideal and elite path. He must fortify his defenses against them, showing their ultimate hollowness, unworthiness, and tendencies to make us complacent (BCA 6.90–100).

Many of these techniques are similar to those practiced by Buddhaghosa, but there are some differences. Śāntideva sometimes encourages himself to hate hatred and to get angry at his anger. Instead of raging at someone who has harmed me, I should hate hatred itself (BCA 6.41). Such powerful emotions have energies that can be therapeutic when skillfully channeled at dismantling their targets (as discussed by Harris 2017). Buddhaghosa, on the other hand, directs all his efforts at diffusing anger and hatred, finding nothing useful in them. Similarly, in other places, Śāntideva suggests harnessing the capacities of what might otherwise be problematic emotions and conditions, like desire, pride, and delight (BCA 7.31–32); in the skillful hands of the practitioner, the energies of such capacities can stimulate one's exertion. Another difference is that Buddhaghosa gives a very elaborate and systematic therapy of the sublime abidings – lovingkindness, compassion, sympathetic joy, and equanimity – but these are mentioned as such only in passing in both of Śāntideva's works. Further, for Śāntideva it is forbearance rather than lovingkindness that serves as the antidote to anger and hatred. Lovingkindness is not showcased as much, and compassion is thematized quite differently, as discussed in the next section.

3.2 Compassion and Understanding

As we have seen in the Four Noble Truths, Buddhist ethical thought begins with the existential problem of suffering and takes it as axiomatic that suffering should be eliminated. For Buddhaghosa, the path of purification slowly and gradually rids one of suffering as one achieves freedom from the afflictions that generate it; this results in a life of nonharming and profound love for others. But for Śāntideva the plight of the world's suffering, and the extraordinary power of the Buddha to ameliorate it, suggest a further calling. The moral path of the aspiring bodhisattva becomes, above all, embracing universal compassion, usually configured as the proactive saving of others. This is a gradual progression of development in which one comes to see one's own liberation and happiness as achieved only through the salvation of others. The bodhisattva comes to be willing to give life and limb to others: The renunciation of self that is generosity frees oneself as it saves others.

We are thus faced with an ethic of radical altruism, which concerns a moral vision to go above and beyond merely refraining from harming others. It is one thing to insist that one stop harming others (as Buddhaghosa does with morality [*sīla*] and the ten moral actions), but altogether another to aim to sacrifice one's body parts or one's own life to ease their distress. Yet this is precisely what Śāntideva comes gradually to ask of himself as he comes to see his own well-being as inextricably interconnected with that of others. To be sure, this ideal is not put in the form of a universal maxim or requirement and so escapes some of the challenges of the demanding moral claims of the sort that Peter Singer, for example, has famously argued for (Singer 1972). Still, universal compassion and its aim to save all beings is Śāntideva's highest vision, and his work seeks to persuade aspiring bodhisattvas that their only true recourse, their only emotionally available option, is to hope to linger for indeterminate future lives saving all beings.

But how does he convince himself and us of this? We have already begun to chronicle some of the main mindfulness techniques that work on the shifts of affect and motivation to reconstruct the psychology of an aspiring bodhisattva. In addition, Śāntideva gives arguments that also do this work, and he considers these arguments as decisive ("there can be no valid objection to the emptiness position" [BCA 9.53]). As Charles Goodman has pointed out, a key verse raised in chapter 8 of *How to Lead an Awakened Life* is also the starting verse of *Training Anthology*:

> When fear and suffering are disliked
> By me and others equally,
> What is so special about me,
> So that I protect myself and not others? (Goodman 2016: lxxiii; BCA 8.96)

In other words, why should I give myself – and not you – special treatment and protection from suffering? The verse thus serves as "an argument for unrestricted impartiality that so many philosophers, both in Asia and in Europe, have identified as a crucial feature of any genuinely moral point of view" (Goodman 2016, xxxviii). For Śāntideva, the rational force of this question commits the aspiring bodhisattva to impartiality as he works to eliminate not just his own suffering but that of all beings. The following verses spell out the reasoning.

> At first one should meditate intently on the equality of oneself and others as follows: "All equally experience suffering and happiness. I should look after them as I do myself."
> Just as the body, with its many parts from division into hands and other limbs, should be protected as a single entity, so too should this entire world which is divided, but undivided in its nature to suffer and be happy.

Even though suffering in me does not cause distress in the bodies of others,
I should nevertheless find their suffering intolerable because of the affection I have for myself.

In the same way that, though I cannot experience another's suffering in myself, his suffering is hard for him to bear because of his affection for himself.

I should dispel the suffering of others because it is suffering like my own suffering. I should help others too because of their nature as beings, which is like my own being (BCA 8.90–95).

These reflections suggest that all beings share suffering and the desire to be happy. Because I share with others the capacity for intolerable pain and misery, it seems arbitrary to recoil at my own pain but not theirs. This is an appeal to the fellowship of all beings in our basic vulnerability to suffering, and it is this empathetic sense of unity that summons the compassionate response of the bodhisattva.[19]

It may not be an entirely successful argument, however, and if we press on it, it is not clear that it holds up. Surely, one might simply point out that the reason I care more about my own suffering than that of others is because my suffering is painful in a crucially important way *for me*, in ways that are not as obviously or necessarily true *for me* when I think of others' suffering. In other words, prioritizing alleviating one's own pain is not inherently irrational. I think a much stronger position would be for Śāntideva to have put the argument in more general terms: Why should I – and not you – get special protection from suffering *by anyone* or *in general*? This is harder to answer. But he puts it in more existential terms: Why should *I* give myself special protection from suffering when others suffer too? And here the answer is all too easy: Because, phenomenologically, my suffering hurts me and it makes obvious sense for me to get rid of it. If these verses are meant to establish impartiality as a universal maxim, they fall short and need buttressing.

They get that buttressing a few verses later in the argument for no-self. No-self teachings – the idea that there is no ultimate self or person beyond the parts and conditions on which conventional notions of person depend – can perhaps do the work of dissolving self-preference:

The continuum of consciousnesses, like a queue, and the combination of constituents, like an army, are not real. The person who experiences suffering does not exist. To whom will that suffering belong?

---

[19] We may recall that Buddhaghosa also offers methods for producing impartiality, most notably "breaking down barriers" where one is not able to turn over to violent brigands any of the four – oneself, a loved one, a neutral, or an enemy. Notice though that this impartiality work is not aimed at a moral purpose and is not advanced as an ethical argument; one breaks down barriers to get rid of the slavery and blindness of one's own hatreds and limitations, not to save all beings.

> If one asks why suffering should be prevented, no one disputes that! If it must
> be prevented, then all of it must be. If not, then this goes for oneself as for
> everyone (BCA 8.101–102).

If the self is dissolved, then there is no basis for self-interest, of putting my
suffering above yours. If there is no person, only constituents (which are also
empty of intrinsic reality), then my preferring my person or self is delusional
and must be abandoned. In this way, Śāntideva begins to turn to the ultimate
teachings about emptiness, particularly for how they dismantle the self and self-
interest; understanding emptiness is needed for impartiality and universal
compassion.

   In both the *Path of Purification* and *How to Lead an Awakened Life*, understanding or wisdom comes at the end of the path, conditioned by the profound
shifts in perception, attention, and feeling that the moral and contemplative
journey make possible; at the same time understanding repeatedly informs
earlier stages of these paths. For Buddhaghosa, understanding (*paññā*) is
"knowing and seeing" without the blinkering blinders of one's own desires,
hatreds, biases, and other limitations. But in Śāntideva's work, understanding
(*prajñā*) is defined by emptiness teachings and emptiness is how one under-
stands reality: "Noble sir, the term 'the way things really are,' 'the way things
really are,' stands for emptiness" (ŚS: 250, with repetition reinforcing the
equivalence). Emptiness means that no term stands independently, nothing
exists by its own intrinsic nature: There is no father, Śāntideva says, without
a son, and vice versa (BCA 9.63–64). This does not mean that fathers and sons
do not exist in *any* sense, but they do not exist independently of each other as
self-contained essential realities because they depend on one another biologi-
cally, socially, and conceptually. In this sense they do not ultimately or intrinsi-
cally exist. Abandoning notions of self-standing essences allows us to see the
radically conditioned and interdependent nature of all things. This teaching
would seem to undermine our fixation on ourselves and support our compassion
for others.

   Many modern scholars working on Śāntideva argue that the metaphysical
stance on emptiness grounds and supports the bodhisattva ethic of compassion (e.g. Garfield 2016): Emptiness can help undergird the bodhisattva's
path, as Śāntideva himself suggests. Having practiced the applications of
mindfulness, he says that one should apply emptiness to everything:

> when the mind is ready in this way, then someone who has the method of full
> Awakening, in order to lift the rest of the living world out of the ocean of
> suffering, and to have power over everything in the three times and to the
> limits of space, should now engage the emptiness of everything. In this way,

the emptiness of the person is attained; and then, because the root has been
cut, reactive emotions do not function (ŚS: 233).

This is to say that understanding emptiness (not just intellectually but in all
ways that one sees and knows) cuts off one's attachments to the "reactive
emotions" that are the toxic defilements. If all things are empty, then there is
no "I" or "mine" to cherish, no "possessions" for me to hoard; my feelings of
anger and hatred and greed are without enduring substance and so can dissolve.
What then can serve as the basis of my attachments and aversions, whereby I put
my needs first and nurture my grievances, desires, needs, partialities? Free from
these I can now "lift the rest of the world out of the ocean of suffering."

But grounding compassion on emptiness also has problems and tensions
even on Śāntideva's own account (as indicated by Williams 1998; Jenkins
2016). For example, Śāntideva himself points out that the insubstantiality of
persons means that the object of one's compassion – the other person – does
not ultimately exist. For whom then does one feel compassion and how does
one help them? He attempts to deal with this problem by suggesting that
projecting the delusion of personhood in this case will make it possible to be
compassionate:

> If you argue: for whom is there compassion if no being exists?
> [Our response is] For anyone projected through the delusion which is
> embraced for the sake of what has to be done (BCA 9.75).

If you do not ultimately exist, how can I help and save you? The answer seems
to be that I can, via *delusion* (*moha*), see that you exist in a conventional sense.
In other words, I have to fall back into delusive conventional notions of persons
to make compassion work. This is worrisome because the entire path is aimed at
dismantling delusion since delusion is a fundamental defilement in Buddhist
thought. Further, it is worth noting that only from a perspective of possessing
ultimate truth might one refer to alternatives as delusional; Śāntideva claims
ultimate truth here.

Still, delusion seems necessary at this point. Not only are you a delusion, but
I do not exist either, ultimately, and I must again rely on delusion to find my
agency as a bodhisattva:

[OBJECTION]   Whose is the task to be done, if there is no being?
[MADHYAMAKA]   True. Moreover, the effort is made in delusion, but in order
                 to bring about an end to suffering, the delusion of what is to
                 be done is not prevented (BCA 9.76).

These verses suggest that far from supporting compassion the ultimate truth of
emptiness makes it much harder going, and that one must resort to delusional

conventional notions of personhood to manage it at all. But have not we been working steadily all along to get rid of such delusions? Have we not been working to deconstruct persons to achieve the ultimate truth that they are empty? And is it not the case that it is only from a standpoint of ultimate truth that we can be certain of what counts as delusional? Yet emptiness removes any sense of concrete personhood that would seem to be required in acts of compassion for concrete others.

There are more troubled waters evident even in Śāntideva's own arguments. Emptiness must apply to suffering as it does to all things, and so suffering too has no enduring, independent, essential reality and cannot exist as such (BCA 9.88, 9.90–91). So the very suffering I am trying to eliminate is in fact ultimately unreal. And, according to emptiness, there is no person who experiences sensation, no bodies, no mind, no subjects of pain (BCA 9.97–101). What then does it mean for me to remove painful sensation, my own or that of others? What is it to give gifts that "have the distinguishing characteristics of illusion and have no intrinsic nature whatsoever"? (ŚS: 258). Further, emptiness applies to all things, so that even samsara and nirvana are not discrete self-existent realities because they depend upon each other for conceptual coherence. In what sense then am I setting out to save unliberated beings? Indeed, if the radical distinction of samsara and nirvana (and path and goal) collapses because both are empty then "all beings are inherently liberated" (BCA 9.103). Why then do they need me?

It seems that to be coherent, the bodhisattva ethic must operate at the level of conventional truth concerning the existence of persons, suffering, compassion, and even samsara and nirvana; and so the practice sits only uneasily with the ultimate truth of emptiness and "the way things really are." Emptiness is useful for dismantling self and ego, which is where so many of our moral problems start, but, as ultimate truth (rather than just a tool), it does not stop there and must apply to all things, dismantling the others whom the bodhisattva sets out to save as well as their suffering. Compassion thus seems to require sailing back into "delusion," which is an odd place to wind up in the chapter on wisdom and ultimate truth attempting to establish a nondelusional grasp of reality.

Traditional commentators and modern scholars have made various efforts to deal with these problems, mostly by attempting to shore up conventional truth in some way, though it is notable that many of those who insist that Śāntideva's metaphysical arguments support his ethics have not always waded into the rapids of chapter 9 to rescue the ethics of compassion from the metaphysical deconstruction of emptiness.[20] Warren Todd offers a reconstruction that

---

[20] Much of the attention to these problems has been focused on the passage in chapter 8 that concerns the problem of "ownerless suffering" discussed where Śāntideva concludes that suffering is bad no matter who owns it and should be eliminated (BCA 8.102–103). On this

suggests that the bodhisattva perches on the edge of both the ultimate reality of emptiness and the conventional reality of ordinary persons and is able to "flicker" back and forth between them to ethical effect; the bodhisattva chooses "voluntary delusion" to embrace a conventional notion of persons and the reality of suffering and compassion to fulfill the vow and does so from a place of higher wisdom of knowing emptiness and the difference between ultimate reality and conventional reality (Todd 2013).

One possible strategy to deal with the ways that the philosophical argumentation advancing the Madhyamaka line too often appears to undermine the ethical position rather than ground it is to suggest that such arguments are meant to be situational meditation strategies, rather than stand-alone metaphysical arguments. William Edelglass has argued that "at the heart of Śāntideva's ethics, then, is the skillful means of discerning what is suitable at any given time" and that his texts are, above all, "meditation manuals" (Edelglass 2017: 245, 227). In this reading, arguments that may fall short of grounding compassion in any final and abstract way might in fact still be useful for the meditator when engaged in specific tasks that are framed within the larger contemplative context of dismantling intuitions of self-interest or preference. This reading of Śāntideva has the support of Śāntideva's own descriptions of his work as "cultivating what is skillful" (BCA 1.3) and as a kind of "training."[21] It suggests that we can profitably read Śāntideva much as I have advocated that we read Buddhaghosa, as employing analytic practices entirely in the service of a therapeutic program and not as offering a stand-alone philosophical tract arguing abstractly for an ethic of salvific compassion. Moreover, Śāntideva sometimes suggests that the kind of analysis the Madhyamaka offers is not intended to issue in a position or basis about reality but rather dismantles any such basis, and there are places in his work where he seems to be disavowing a final metaphysical position: "But when the thing which is to be analyzed has been analyzed there is no basis left for analysis. Since there is no basis it does not continue and that is said to be Enlightenment" (BCA 9.110).

Though largely sympathetic to this style of reading, I think that the sort of epistemological and metaphysical argumentation that we get in chapter 9 of BCA draws on, rehearses, and is framed by long-standing philosophical

---

passage and possible interpretations, see Williams 1998; Cowherds 2016 (especially the articles by Garfield, Jenkins, and Priest; Garfield; and Westerhoff); and Finnegan 2018. What is surprising is the lack of attention (with the exception of Todd 2013) to similar but even more difficult ideas laid out in chapter 9 that I have only briefly indicated here.

[21] There are good reasons not to treat Buddhist texts as "purportedly detached descriptions of metaphysical truth espoused by academic philosophers," as suggested by Rafal Stepien (2018: 1088), but instead as what they purport to be – pragmatic soteriological projects.

argumentation that Śāntideva uses as the basis of his therapeutic program in the first place. As we have seen, Śāntideva is exclusivist about the "emptiness position" and he holds this on the basis of what he takes to be the persuasiveness of his tradition's arguments, which he then recapitulates in his own works. Further, his views on what exactly "understanding" (*prajñā*, the topic of chapter 9) consists of differ than Buddhaghosa's *paññā*; whereas for Buddhaghosa it consists of methods of analysis derived from scripture but not advanced via epistemological or metaphysical argumentation, for Śāntideva it consists of removing wrong view via philosophical debates with other positions, debates that aim at convincing others of their merits. Moreover, Śāntideva's vision of compassion is of a radical and demanding sort, one that we may reasonably look to see strong arguments marshaled to support. Standing at the pinnacle of centuries of rigorous philosophical debate on which he rests his ideals, Śāntideva might reasonably be expected to demonstrate how the two highest values in the Madhyamaka tradition – emptiness and compassion – consistently support one another.

In Buddhaghosa's case, we do not have to struggle with places where emptiness does not support compassion and lovingkindness because Buddhaghosa uses emptiness as just one tool among others as a meditation practice for particular purposes in specific contexts. Emptiness is never advanced as an exclusivist position that requires argumentation to support. (Whether this makes him a stronger philosopher or a weaker one is for the reader to decide.) He uses emptiness and no-self teachings in a targeted fashion to dismantle selves and phenomena to counter our tendencies to essentialize and reify them; but he can put down these tools when he turns to the sublime abidings, which make use of the Buddha's conventional teachings about persons. It is unclear to me how Śāntideva can recommend setting aside emptiness, even when it makes persons, suffering, compassion, and action "empty" in ways that challenge what compassionate action can actually mean – unless of course one takes recourse in "delusion." Because Buddhaghosa does not argue in general terms for emptiness as ultimate truth (indeed, he does not argue for any sort of ultimate truth or reality), he does not have to cope with it when it becomes inconvenient, as when we need to look upon concrete and particular persons in compassion, to see them in their personhood, to recognize that their suffering is real, and to offer concrete help. In those contexts, as he has said all along, the Buddha's more conventional teachings are far more useful. And no less true.

3.3 Extreme Altruism and Living in the World

We have seen that Śāntideva's bodhisattva ethic, by advocating bodily sacrifice and radical acts of generosity as the very practices that bring about one's own awakening, goes further than Buddhaghosa's nonharming and impartial love and compassion. Buddhists have numerous stories celebrating the Buddha's gifts of the body wherein, as a bodhisattva training in generosity, he plucks out his eyes to allow a blind person to see or offers his body to feed the hungry. A bodhisattva is committed, as we saw in Śāntideva's initial vows, to "become both food and drink" for the famished and to make over his "body to all embodied beings." And *Training Anthology* describes lavish bodhisattva gifts not only of possessions and service to the needy, but of body parts and, indeed, life itself. Śāntideva's vision of renunciation and compassion is so thoroughgoing that it requires abandoning all residual attachment to possessions, body, and oneself as realized and displayed in such giving.

In places the bodhisattvas' munificence seems extravagant, hyperbolic, and perhaps even a tad perverse: Not content to offer their humble service to beggars, bodhisattvas should offer them their ears and noses; asked for their tongues, they happily rip them out and offer them; even giving their heads to others simply yields more opportunities for enjoying "pristine awareness" (ŚS: 26–27). (Flores 2008 offers a subtle literary reading of the motives and ideology behind these magnificent gestures). Yet there are other places in his texts where Śāntideva becomes surprisingly circumspect about such munificent giving, and sometimes it does not seem to be so unconditional as it might first appear. For example, one should sacrifice one's life only for someone equally or more compassionate than one is, for then there is no "overall loss" to the world of a supremely compassionate person (BCA 5.87). But who can really be as compassionate as a bodhisattva? (Is it unjust to allege a whiff of the pride and supremacy in the bodhisattva's mission that elsewhere Śāntideva struggles so valiantly to excise?) At other times we find Śāntideva quoting from texts that enjoin the bodhisattva to protect the Dharma by practicing in solitude and avoiding all sorts of people including "untouchables, boxers, bartenders, and non-Buddhists," immoral monks, nuns who laugh and chatter, intersex persons, dancers, athletes, musicians, those believed by others to be *arhats*, and even laypeople (ŚS: 52); elsewhere, it is advisable to avoid "uneducated people" (106). On the other hand, Śāntideva quotes another text that urges bodhisattvas to not become too comfortable in solitary seclusion because avoiding others does not allow for working on the defilements, and "in this way, they neither practice for their own benefit nor for the benefit of others" (ŚS: 53). Difficult people, as we have seen, actually offer means for developing one's practice (BCA 6.102–108).

We might also subject Śāntideva's moral treatise to ethical scrutiny for its treatment of women. On the one hand, women can become bodhisattvas and follow this extraordinary path (ŚS: 14). On the other hand, the ideal bodhisattva imagined in his texts is a male monastic; we have only one example of an advanced female bodhisattva among many male bodhisattvas, and she is treated with some ambivalence (Mrozik 2007: 56–69). The texts presume and in many cases *reinforce* Buddhist social and often highly essentialist assumptions about gender. Women are objects that can be given away as gifts by a bodhisattva (ŚS: 26); they represent dangerous and wanton threats to male celibacy and peace of mind (ŚS: 76; 84–84, for example); and a female birth (and thus life) is ranked lower in moral and spiritual capacity than birth as a male.

Goodman notes with regard to some of these issues of gender that "all of Śāntideva's brilliant reflections on the structure of moral reasons unfold within confines established by sacred scriptures that take the social system of India mostly for granted" (2016, xli). Although emptiness teachings sometimes break down essentialist constructions of women and gender for the purposes of dismantling male lust, such teachings are *not* deployed to break down social hierarchy and stereotypes (and these have been highly consequential in the institutional history of gender inequality in Buddhism). In fact, in chapter 9 of *How to Lead an Awakened Life*, where the highest wisdom on emptiness and ultimate truth is said to emerge, Śāntideva explicitly affirms that "spiritually developed" people "understand reality better than ordinary people do," and so can contravene "the ordinary definition that women are not impure" – in other words, spiritually developed people affirm that women are impure![22] Given that Śāntideva possessed (and extolled in the highest possible terms) the resources to disrupt essentialist definitions about people, and that he claimed both access to ultimate truth and a maximalist moral ethic of generosity and compassion, it remains an important scholarly and ethical question for us to consider whether we are entitled to hold him to account for not deploying these to dismantle and reconsider the social categories and ideologies of his time. Of course, no thinker stands outside of his or her historical context and social conditioning (Buddhaghosa also assumed a patriarchal worldview). But those who would make claims about maximalist ethical perfection and the possession of ultimate truth beyond all conventional distinctions surely open themselves to ethical scrutiny when they promote their prejudices as the wise knowing of the spiritually developed.

These considerations are the stuff of honest intellectual and ethical engagement as we take Śāntideva as a thinker serious enough to address us. Buddhist

---

[22] The verse reads (in Crosby and Skilton's translation): "there is no fault in the use of conventional truth by the spiritually developed. They understand reality better than ordinary people do. Otherwise ordinary people would invalidate the definition of women as impure" (BCA 9.8). Some of the context here: In verse 9.3 we have been told that "the worldview of the undeveloped is invalidated by the world view of the spiritually developed," and in verse 9.6 we learn that consensus of ordinary people can be wrong, as "for example, the popular view that impure things are pure."

thinkers are not antiquities or museum pieces to look at for their interesting but largely irrelevant world views. They can become our interlocutors with something to teach us, but as they do we must probe their strengths and limitations. In the case of Śāntideva, his extraordinary capacity to hold in view simultaneously the depths of human depravity and the soaring heights of compassionate moral concern has made him one of the most inspiring thinkers in Buddhist history. And his vision and articulation of the moral and emancipatory work of dismantling essentialism, although imperfectly wielded, may offer people everywhere valuable resources for the ethical demands of identifying and seeing beyond the false constructions of our own biases.

4 Conclusions

Scholars disagree about whether Śāntideva's extravagant moral vision finds full philosophical support in his arguments about emptiness. It remains a matter of dispute whether ultimate teachings of emptiness and no-self are necessary conditions for the practice of universal compassion, or, conversely, hindrances to it. It also remains an open question, indeed one further raised by Buddhaghosa's work, whether metaphysical arguments are necessary in any way for pragmatic and programmatic moral reflection and action given that Buddhaghosa manages these without them. In any case, reading these two thinkers together has helped sharpen these two different approaches available within Buddhist thinking, some of which may be usefully recapped here.

Buddhaghosa's approach is less ambitious than Śāntideva's in two main respects. First, Buddhaghosa's ideal is considerably less exalted; not for him the moral ideal of the radically altruistic and forever-committed bodhisattva of universal compassion. To be sure, the aspiring *arhat* is hardly a slouch, as indicated by Buddhaghosa's arduous and painstaking techniques for ridding oneself one-by-one of harmful defilements. And their aims differ: The aspiring *arhat* seeks, above all, freedom, and freedom, above all, from one's own defilements. Ridding oneself of hatred, pride, greed, and anger is not a moral injunction so much as a prudential matter of seeking liberation, although it might have valuable moral side effects in that, when defilements are removed, harmful actions are impossible and love and compassion become immeasurable. Śāntideva, on the other hand, finds the highest aspiration of the Buddhist path to require universal compassion of saving others; the highest therapy of liberating oneself requires, at bottom, actively addressing the needs and suffering of others.

But for extraordinary moral visions much philosophical support is demanded, and here we see the second way that Śāntideva's position is more ambitious than Buddhaghosa's program. Śāntideva must argue why the bodhisattva ideal is the only rational course for him – and others – to pursue. So he develops a notion of ultimate truth that dismantles self to undergird the impartiality ethic of universal compassion. But, as we have seen, for some scholars this effort does not fully succeed, because to practice compassion as anything other than a lofty abstraction would seem to require a concrete notion of persons – a notion that Śāntideva has told us is "delusional." Whether and how the bodhisattva is able to negotiate consistently or simultaneously the ultimate realization of emptiness and the practical matter of actually helping persons is not satisfactorily resolved in the texts that we have from Śāntideva, despite various modern scholarly attempts to shore things up.

In this sense, Buddhaghosa's less exalted vision and more pragmatic efforts to cope systematically with one's phenomenological condition, moment-by-moment, in the context of living one's life, spared him the onus of metaphysical argumentation to support it. The price may be universalist ethical claims, of course, but free of the need to argue for such claims, he can set about deploying Buddhist doctrines (like emptiness and no-self) not as universal truths but, more pragmatically, as tools of disciplinary and therapeutic analysis to change, in truly extraordinary ways, human experience.

References

Bodhi, Bhikkhu, trans. (2015). *In the Buddha's Words: An Anthology of Discourses from the Pāli Canon.* Somerville, MA: Wisdom Publications.

Bronkhorst, Johannes. (2018). "Abhidharma in Early Mahāyāna." In *Setting out on the Great Way,* ed. Paul Harrison. Sheffield: Equinox, 119–140.

Clayton, Barbra. (2006). *Moral Theory in Śāntideva's Śikṣāsamuccaya: Cultivating the Fruits of Virtue.* London: Routledge.

Clayton, Barbra. (2009). "Śāntideva, Virtue, Consequentialism." In *Destroying Māra Forever: Buddhist Ethics Essays in Honor of Damien Keown,* eds. John Powers and Charles S. Prebish. Ithaca, NY: Snow Lion Publications, 15–29.

Cozort, Daniel and James Mark Shields, eds. (2018). *The Oxford Handbook of Buddhist Ethics.* Oxford: Oxford University Press.

Crosby, Kate, and Skilton, Andrew, trans. *Śāntideva, The Bodhicaryāvatāra.* Oxford: Oxford University Press, 2008.

Desjarlais, Robert. (2003). *Sensory Biographies: Lives and Deaths among Nepal's Yolmo Buddhists.* Berkeley, CA: University of California Press.

Dreyfus Georges. (1995). "Meditation as Ethical Activity." *Journal of Buddhist Ethics,* 2, 28–54.

"The Dhammapada: A Translation", translated from the Pali by Thanissaro Bhikkhu. Access to Insight (BCBS Edition), 30 November 2013, http://www.accesstoinsight.org/tipitaka/kn/dhp/dhp.intro.than.html.

Eberhardt, Nancy. (2006). *Imagining the Course of Life: Self-transformation in a Shan Buddhist Community.* Honolulu, HI: University of Hawai'i Press.

Edelglass, William. (2013). "Buddhist Ethics and Western Moral Philosophy." In *A Companion to Buddhist Philosophy,* ed. Steven M. Emmanuel. West Sussex: John Wiley & Sons, 476–490.

Edelglass, William. (2017). "Mindfulness and Moral Transformation: Awakening to Others in Śāntideva's Ethics." In *The Bloomsbury Research Handbook of Indian Ethics,* ed. Shyam Ranganathan. London: Bloomsbury, 225–248.

Emmanuel, Steven, ed. (2013). *A Companion to Buddhist Philosophy.* West Sussex: John Wiley & Sons.

Finnegan, Bronwyn. (2018). "Madhyamaka Ethics." In *The Oxford Handbook of Buddhist Ethics,* eds. Daniel Cozort and James Mark Shields. Oxford: Oxford University Press, 162–183.

Fiordalis, David, ed. (2018). *Buddhist Spiritual Practices: Thinking with Pierre Hadot on Buddhism, Philosophy, and the Path*. Berkeley, CA: Mangalam Press.

Flores, Ralph. (2008). *Buddhist Scriptures as Literature: Sacred Rhetoric and the Uses of Theory*. Albany: State University of New York Press.

Foucault, Michel. (1997). *Ethics, Subjectivity, and Truth*, ed. Paul Rabinow; trans. Robert Hurley et. al. New York: The New Press.

Ganeri, Jonardon. (2017). *Attention, Not Self*. Oxford: Oxford University Press.

Ganeri Jonardon and Carlisle Clare. (2010). *Philosophy as Therapeia*. Royal Institute of Philosophy Supplement: 66. Cambridge: Cambridge University Press.

Garfield, Jay. (2002). *Empty Words: Buddhist Philosophy and Cross-Cultural Interpretation*. Oxford: Oxford University Press.

Garfield, Jay. (2010). "What is it like to be a Bodhisattva? Moral Phenomenology in Śāntideva's *Bodhicaryāvatāra*." *The Journal of the International Association of Buddhist Studies* 33(1–2), 333–357.

Garfield, Jay. (2016). "Buddhist Ethics in the Context of Conventional Truth." In *Moonpaths: Ethics and Emptiness*, ed. The Cowherds. New York: Oxford University Press, 77–95.

Garfield, Jay, Stephen Jenkins, and Graham Priest. (2016). "The Śāntideva Passage: *Bodhicaryāvatāra* VIII.90–103, 55." In *Moonpaths: Ethics and Emptiness*, ed. The Cowherds. New York: Oxford University Press, 55–76.

Gethin, Rupert. (1998). *The Foundations of Buddhism*. Oxford: Oxford University Press.

Gomez, Luis. (1976). "Proto-Mādhyamaka in the Pāli Canon." *Philosophy East and West* 26(2), 137–165.

Goodman, Charles. (2009). *Consequences of Compassion: An Interpretation and Defense of Buddhist Ethics*. New York: Oxford University Press.

Goodman, Charles, trans. (2016). *The Training Anthology of Śāntideva: A Translation of the Śikṣā-samuccaya*. New York: Oxford University Press.

Gowans, Christopher. (2013). "Ethical Thought in Indian Buddhism." In *A Companion to Buddhist Philosophy*, ed. Steven M. Emmanuel. West Sussex: John Wiley & Sons, 429–451.

Gyatso, Tenzin (Dalai Lama XIV). (1999). *Ethics for the New Millennium*. New York: Riverhead Books.

Gyatso, Tenzin (Dalai Lama XIV). (2009). *For the Benefit of All Beings: A Commentary on the Way of the Bodhisattva*. Boston: Shambhala.

Gyatso, Tenzin (Dalai Lama XIV) and Jinpa Thupten. (2005). *Practicing Wisdom: The Perfection of Shantideva's Bodhisattva Way*. Boston: Wisdom Publications.

Hadot, Pierre. (1995). *Philosophy as a Way of Life: Spiritual Exercise from Socrates to Foucault*, ed. Arnold I. Davison; trans. Michael Chase. Malden, MA: Blackwell Publishing, 1995.

Hallisey, Charles. (1996). "Ethical Particularism in Theravāda Buddhism. *Journal of Buddhist Ethics*, 3, 32–43.

Harris, Stephen E. (2015). "On the Classification of Śāntideva's Ethics in the *Bodhicaryāvatāra.*" *Philosophy East and West* 65(1), 249–275.

Harris, Stephen E. (2017). "The Skillful Handling of Poison: *Bodhicitta* and the *Kleśas* in Śāntideva's *Bodhicaryāvatāra*. *Journal of Indian Philosophy* 45(2), 331–348.

Heim, Maria. (2006) "Toward a Wider and Juster Initiative: Recent Comparative Work in Buddhist Ethics." *Religion Compass* 1, 1–13.

Heim, M. (2014) *The Forerunner of All Things: Buddhaghosa on Mind, Intention, and Agency*. New York: Oxford University Press.

Heim, Maria. (2017). "Buddhaghosa on the Phenomenology of Love and Compassion." In *The Oxford Handbook of Indian Philosophy*, ed. Jonardon Ganeri. New York: Oxford University Press, 171–189.

Heim, Maria. (2018). *Voice of the Buddha: Buddhaghosa on the Immeasurable Words*. New York: Oxford University Press.

Heim, Maria. (forthcoming). "The Perfectly-Awakened Buddha, the First Abhidhammikas, and the *Dhammasaṅgaṇī* and *Vibhaṅga.*" In *The Routledge Handbook of Indian Buddhist Philosophy*, eds. William Edelglass, Pierre-Julien Herter, and Sara McClintock. New York: Routledge.

Heim, Maria, and Chakravarthi Ram-Prasad. (2018). "In a Double Way: *Nāma-Rūpa* in Buddhaghosa's Phenomenology." *Philosophy East and West* 68(4), 1085–1115.

Jenkins, Stephen. 2016. "Waking into Compassion: The Three *Ālambana* of *Karuṇā.*" In Cowherds (eds), *Moonpaths: Ethics and Emptiness*. New York: Oxford University Press. 97–118.

Kapstein, Michael. (2013). "Stoics and Bodhisattvas: Spiritual Exercises and Faith in Two Philosophical Traditions." In *Philosophy as a Way of Life: Ancient and Modern – Essays in Honor of Pierre Hadot*, eds. Michael Chase, Stephen R. L. Clark, and Michael McGhee. Hoboken: John Wiley & Sons, 99–115.

Keown, Damien. (1992). *The Nature of Buddhist Ethics*. New York: Palgrave.

Keown, Damien. (2005). *Buddhist Ethics: A Very Short Introduction*. New York: Oxford University Press.

King, Sallie. (2009). *Socially Engaged Buddhism*. Honolulu: University of Hawai'i Press.

Lele, Amod. (2015). "The Metaphysical Basis of Śāntideva's Ethics." *Journal of Buddhist Ethics* 22, 249–283.

McRae, Emily. (2015). "Buddhist Therapies of the Emotions and the Psychology of Moral Improvement." *History of Philosophy Quarterly* 32 (3), 101–122.

McRae, Emily. (2018). "The Psychology of Moral Judgement and Perception in Indo-Tibetan Buddhist Ethics." In *The Oxford Handbook of Buddhist Ethics*, eds. Daniel Cozort and James Mark Shields. Oxford: Oxford University Press, 335–358.

Mrozik, Susanne. (2007). *Virtuous Bodies: The Physical Dimensions of Morality in Buddhist Ethics*. New York: Oxford University Press.

Murdoch, Iris. (1971). *The Sovereignty of Good*. London: Routledge.

Ñāṇamoli, Bhikkhu and Bodhi, Bhikkhu, trans. (2001). *The Middle Length Discourses of the Buddha: A Translation of the Majjhima Nikāya*. Boston: Wisdom Publications.

Ñāṇamoli, Bhikkhu, trans. (1975). *The Path of Purification (Visuddhimagga) by Bhadantācariya Buddhaghosa*. Kandy, Sri Lanka: Buddhist Publication Society.

Ñāṇamoli, Bhikkhu, trans. (1982). *The Path of Discrimination (Paṭisambhidāmagga)*. London.

Ñāṇamoli, Bhikkhu, trans. (1996). *The Dispeller of Delusion (Sammohavinodanī)*. Revised for publication by L. S. Cousins, Nyanaponika Mahāthera, and C. M. M. Shaw. Oxford: Pali Text Society.

Ñāṇamoli, Bhikkhu, and Bhikkhu Bodhi, trans. (1991). *The Discourse on Right View: The Sammādiṭṭhi Sutta and its Commentary*. Kandy, Sri Lanka: Buddhist Publication Society.

Ñāṇamoli, Bhikkhu, and Bhikkhu Bodhi, trans. (1995). *The Middle-Length Discourses of the Buddha: A Translation of the Majjhima Nikāya*. Somerville, MA: Wisdom Publications.

Nussbaum, Martha. (1994). *Therapies of Desire: Theory and Practice in Hellenistic Ethics*. Princeton: Princeton University Press.

Nussbaum, Martha. (2001). *Upheavals of Thought: The Intelligence of Emotions*. Cambridge: Cambridge University Press.

Pe Maung Tin, trans.; ed. Caroline Rhys Davids. (1999). *The Expositor (Atthasālinī)*. Oxford: Pali Text Society.

Queen, Christopher, and King, Sallie. (1996). *Engaged Buddhism: Buddhist Liberation Movements in Asia*. Albany, NY: State University of New York Press.

Ram-Prasad, Chakravarthi. (2018). *Human Being, Bodily Being*. London: Oxford University Press.

Rhys Davids, A. F. Caroline. (1975) *A Buddhist Manual of Psychological Ethics (Dhammasaṅgaṇī)*. London: Royal Asiatic Society.

Siderits, Mark. (2016). "Does 'Buddhist Ethics' Exist?" In *Moonpaths: Ethics and Emptiness*, eds. The Cowherds. New York: Oxford University Press, 119–39.

Singer, Peter. (1972). "Famine, Affluence, and Morality." *Philosophy and Public Affairs* 1(3), 229–243.

Stepien, Rafal. (2018). "Orienting Reason: A Religious Critique of Philosophizing Nāgārjuna." *Journal of the American Academy of Religion* 86(4), 1072–1106.

The Cowherds. (2016). *Moonpaths: Ethics and Emptiness*. New York: Oxford University Press.

Todd, Warren, (2013). *The Ethics of Śaṅkara and Śāntideva: A Selfless Response to an Illusory World*. Burlington: Ashgate.

Vélez de Cea, Abraham. (2004). "The Criteria of Goodness in the Pāli Nikāyas and the Nature of Buddhist Ethics." *Journal of Buddhist Ethics* 11, 123–142.

Vasen, Sīlavādin Meynard. (2018). "Buddhist Ethics Compared to Western Ethics." In *The Oxford Handbook of Buddhist Ethics*, eds. Daniel Cozort and James Mark Shields. Oxford: Oxford University Press, 317–334.

Walshe, Maurice, trans. (1995). *The Long Discourses of the Buddha: A Translation of the Dīgha Nikāya*. Boston: Wisdom Publications.

Westerhoff, Jan. (2016). "The Connection Between Ontology and Ethics in Madhyamaka Thought." In *Moonpaths: Ethics and Emptiness*, eds. The Cowherds. New York: Oxford University Press, 203–220.

Williams, Paul. (1998). *Altruism and Reality: Studies in the Philosophy of the Bodhicaryāvatāra*, New York: Routledge.

Acknowledgments

This approach to Buddhist ethics by focusing on Buddhaghosa and Śāntideva was inspired by conversations with Jay Garfield and his putting together a panel on both thinkers for the American Academy of Religion in Denver, 2018. I am grateful to him and to the other panelists, Amber Carpenter, Stephen Harris, Emily McRae, Guy Newland, and Sonam Thakchöe, for a rich discussion that helped sharpen some of my thinking of this comparison. My extreme gratitude also to Steve Heim, Chakravarthi Ram-Prasad, and William Edelglass for reading drafts of the manuscript and offering much invaluable advice for its improvement.

Cambridge Elements ☰

Elements in Ethics

Ben Eggleston
University of Kansas

Ben Eggleston is a professor of philosophy at the University of Kansas. He is the editor of John Stuart Mill, *Utilitarianism: With Related Remarks from Mill's Other Writings* (Hackett, 2017) and a co-editor of *Moral Theory and Climate Change: Ethical Perspectives on a Warming Planet* (Routledge, 2020), *The Cambridge Companion to Utilitarianism* (Cambridge, 2014), and *John Stuart Mill and the Art of Life* (Oxford, 2011). He is also the author of numerous articles and book chapters on various topics in ethics.

Dale E. Miller
Old Dominion University, Virginia

Dale E. Miller is a professor of philosophy at Old Dominion University. He is the author of *John Stuart Mill: Moral, Social and Political Thought* (Polity, 2010) and a co-editor of *Moral Theory and Climate Change: Ethical Perspectives on a Warming Planet* (Routledge, 2020), *A Companion to Mill* (Blackwell, 2017), *The Cambridge Companion to Utilitarianism* (Cambridge, 2014), *John Stuart Mill and the Art of Life* (Oxford, 2011), and *Morality, Rules, and Consequences: A Critical Reader* (Edinburgh, 2000). He is also the editor-in-chief of *Utilitas*, and the author of numerous articles and book chapters on various topics in ethics broadly construed.

About the Series

This Elements series provides an extensive overview of major figures, theories, and concepts in the field of ethics. Each entry in the series acquaints students with the main aspects of its topic while articulating the author's distinctive viewpoint in a manner that will interest researchers.

Cambridge Elements ≡

Elements in Ethics